Michigan
Real Estate
EXAM
PREP

The SMART Guide to Passing

Marge Fraser
GRI, ABR

THOMSON
━━━━━✦━━━━━ ™
SOUTH-WESTERN

Australia · Brazil · Canada · Mexico · Singapore · Spain · United Kingdom · United States

THOMSON

SOUTH-WESTERN

**Michigan Real Estate Exam Prep:
The Smart Guide to Passing, First Edition**

Thomson

Prepared by Marge Fraser

VP/Editorial Director:
Jack W. Calhoun

VP/Editor-in-Chief:
Dave Shaut

Executive Editor: Scott Person:
Daniel Jones

Associate Acquisitions Editor:
Sara Glassmeyer

Outside Development Services:
Margaret Maloney

Associate Content Project Manager:
Joanna Grote

Manager of Technology, Editorial:
Vicky True

Senior Technology Project Manager:
Matt McKinney

Senior Technology Project Manager:
Matt McKinney

Senior Manufacturing Communications Manager:
Jim Overly

Senior Manufacturing Coordinator:
Doug Wilke

Art Director:
Linda Helcher

Cover Designer:
Pop Design Works

Printer:
West
Eagan, Minnesota

Library of Congress Control Number:
2006907268

For more information about our products,
contact us at:

Thomson Learning Academic Resource
Center

1-800-423-0563

Thomson Higher Education
5191 Natorp Boulevard
Mason, OH 45040
USA

The author would like to thank the following reviewer for his comments and suggestions:

Daniel Alter – Sterling Heights, Michigan

CONTENTS

4

Introduction

Additional exposure to the material and repetition will improve your confidence and help alleviate "exam anxiety." The more you know, the less stress you will have when taking the test. There is no magic wand or "smart pill" you can take, but if you follow these guidelines, we think you will be successful.

General Study Hints

Use questions in your book more than once. Write your answers on a separate sheet of paper. This will make scoring easier as you compare your answers with the answer key in the back of the booklet, and leave the questions unmarked for additional "practice" retakes. This will also work with your regular textbook and any other practice exams you might decide to use.

Practice taking timed tests. Duplicate the testing situation by practicing the questions under pressure. This is one of the best ways to overcome exam anxiety. Based on the time allowed on the state examination, your goal should be to complete 50 questions per hour. Missed items quickly pinpoint your weak areas and help focus your attention on them for additional study.

Research wrong answers. First, carefully read the explanation in the answer key. Determine why the correct answer is correct and the other "distracters" are not. Try not to memorize individual questions, as this may cause you to miss subtle wording differences on the exam, thereby causing you to answer incorrectly. You need to concentrate on concepts, not exact phrasing.

Pace your studying. Immediately test yourself after class discussion. Look up wrong answers. Remember that last-minute cramming before a final exam or the state licensing exam may cause you to panic when confronted with difficult material or to become overly tired during the exam. Do not get behind in your studying; it is difficult to catch up.

Limit your study time. Most people more easily recall the first and last part of whatever they study, while the middle material becomes a little muddled. It is better to study for 10 to 20 minutes with breaks rather than for a solid hour.

Get a good night's sleep before the test. A proper amount of sleep will help you think more clearly and avoid errors from just being tired. "Pulling an all nighter" will just make you tired and often more confused.

Know where you are going. If you are going to a test site in another town, know how to get there and give yourself lots of extra time. Do not add to your frustration by being late!

Know the testing rules. Review your examination guide to be sure you know how you will be tested and the general process. There are generally a few sample questions in the guide, as well as a list of content to be tested. There should also be a chart of how many questions will be asked in each general category.

Last-minute study. Your last-minute study should include definitions from your regular text for the national portion and the key point review for the Michigan portion from this booklet. If you struggle with a given topic, don't waste time trying to master it at the very end. Move on and review the material with which you are more familiar.

If you are just beginning your class, try these additional tips:

1. Read the assigned material BEFORE class. If you are in a classroom setting, then the lecture should help reinforce what you have read. Highlight what you think are important points and jot down any questions you might need to ask. Don't highlight everything in your book! Hold your questions until the topic is completed as your question may be answered during the lecture. If ever unsure about asking, speak with the instructor during a break.
2. Participate, don't just talk. Instructors enjoy well-asked questions that give them an opportunity to "teach." However, no one enjoys a classroom where students are continually talking to each other or telling "war stories" that have little to do with the topic.
3. Organize your notes and handouts. Many students accumulate a lot of paper during a class, and it quickly becomes unorganized. Consider using a 3-ring binder or a folder with pockets to stay organized.
4. If you are in a live class, be on time and always listen for instructions. Being late a time or two or daydreaming during class may mean missing a question or two. Those missed items could make the difference between passing and failing.

Test Taking Strategies

1. **Read the question.** Some students go so far as putting a huge "RTQ" on some scratch paper to remind them! It is imperative to know what is being asked. Look for words like NOT or EXCEPT or INCORRECT. In math questions, the numbers provided may be monthly, but the question is seeking an annual number. Make sure you understand the question before you look at the answers!

2. **Read the answers.** Go through the 4 choices. Look for ones that can be easily eliminated. Some students put "A B C D" on a sheet of paper for tougher questions and physically mark through incorrect answers as they are eliminated. If you can eliminate 2 answers, you now have a 50-50 chance, even if you have to guess! You might want to approach a multiple choice question as 4 separate True/False questions — you are looking for the True answer. On questions with two Yes and two No answers, be sure to read what follows the Yes and No, as that is usually the key to answering correctly.

3. **Review your answer.** When done, review by reading the question and the answer you picked, asking yourself, "Does this completed sentence make sense?" If it is a "story problem," put yourself in the story. Does the correct answer make common sense to you? On math problems, put the answer back into the formula. Also, is the answer logical? It wouldn't make sense for a $100,000 home to have annual real estate taxes of $50,000.

4. **Make sure you immediately record your answer.** Many students find that silly mistakes, such as recording "B" instead of "D" on their answer sheet, will cost them a point or two.

5. **Manage your time during the exam.** Go through the entire exam in order, answering the questions that come easily. If you are in doubt or do not know the answer, skip it and move on. Many students use 45–60 minutes to answer about 70% of the questions. This leaves plenty of time to focus on the remaining 30%. On computerized exams, there should be an indicator of how many questions have been answered and how much time is remaining.

6. **Manage your panic.** Better yet, don't panic! As you go through the exam the first time, remember that it is normal to leave about one out of four questions blank. When you come to a question that stumps you, remember that subsequent questions may jog your memory or provide answers to earlier questions; look for that help. Remember that you can miss 1 of every 4 questions and still pass.

7. **Stay comfortable and avoid stress.** Lean back in your chair and roll your neck occasionally. If necessary, get up and stretch or use the restroom. Staying comfortable will help you stay focused on the test itself. By the way, the small camera that may be on top of your computer station is there to take your picture for licensing — it is not there spying and constantly watching you as some students believe!

8. **Math problems.** Keep all of your work for each problem in one area, circle the work, and label it with a number. That way, you can quickly review your work if needed. Start by developing the formula. For example, on a tax question you might want to write down:

Assessed Value x Tax Rate = $Taxes Paid

You will always be given two of the numbers and be asked to solve for the third:
50,000 x Tax Rate = $4,000.

To solve this formula, the $4,000 is divided by 50,000 to obtain the correct answer. However, if you panic and forget how to solve it from this point, you can replace the Tax Rate with all 4 possible answers to see which one works. Regardless, make sure your selected answer will fit into the formula and produce the correct answer.

It is possible to calculate an incorrect answer that matches one of the answers on the inches to feet, or feet to yards, misplace a decimal point, or similar common mistakes. Don't lose points over simply being careless or sloppy.

9. **Don't get stuck on any one question or problem.** Rather than dwell on a single problem, you could be answering several more questions to which you DO know the answer. Also, a later question may provide you with a clue or answer to the bypassed one. Get out of negative thinking and move on to the next question!

10. **Don't change an answer.** Unless you find an obvious mistake, such as an incorrectly recorded answer or misread question, do NOT change your original response. First instincts are correct more often than changed answers. Be 100% sure if you are going to make a change.

11. **Answer all questions.** Before handing your test in, or indicating on your computer that you are finished, be sure every question as an answer. If you are out of time, mark one answer for each randomly. It can only help your score.

12. **Congratulations — you've passed!** If so, you may want to let your instructor know. If you fail for some reason, before leaving the test site, write down questions or areas that need more study. You may forget many of these if you wait until you get home.

Examination Content Outline

Topic	Number of Questions	
	Salesperson	**Broker**
Listing Property	22	17
Selling Property	20	16
Property Management	9	13
Settlement/Transfer of Ownership	1 3	15
Financing	21	18
Professional Responsibilities/Fair Practice/Administration	15	21
Michigan State Laws and Rules		
Duties and Powers	3	3
Licensing Requirements	3	3
Statutory Requirements	10	13
Additional State Topics	<u>14</u>	<u>16</u>
Total Scored Items	130	135
Pre-Test Items (maximum)	10	10

KEY POINT REVIEW

The following are key exam concepts that make a great final study guide for the real estate licensing exam. The key points are intentionally short and to the point to make them easier to understand and absorb. They are organized by the topics/laws as tested on the Michigan section of the licensing exam.

Introduction to Real Estate Principles

1. Real property includes the surface of the land, improvements attached to the land, minerals beneath the surface, and air space above the land.

2. Everything that is not real property is personal property. Tangible personal property is readily movable.

3. Real property has the physical characteristics of immobility (land cannot be relocated), indestructibility (land cannot be destroyed), and uniqueness (no two parcels of land are identical).

4. Real property has unique economic characteristics based on scarcity (the lower the supply, the greater the demand), permanence of investment (land can not be moved so the investment does not diminish), location (the greatest affect on value), and improvements (adding improvements on the land such as electric, gas, etc., and adding improvements to the land such as grading, landscaping, buildings, etc.).

5. Land use controls are found both in both private deed restrictions and public laws.

6. The real estate profession involves many specialties other than residential sales and requires knowledge in areas such as financing, housing codes, and other related fields.

7. The real estate profession is organized at local, state, and national levels primarily through the National Association of REALTORS®.

8. A real estate market is local in nature and is a good example of the free-market concept.

9. The greatest use of the land is considered its highest and best use.

10. The feudal system of land ownership allowed the land to be owned only by the ruling powers. Our system of land ownership today, which allows private ownership of land, is referred to as the allodial system.

11. Real estate licensees act as advisors to their clients and customers. Because a home's sale and purchase often involve the seller's most important financial asset and create long-term financial obligations for the buyer, licensees have to be thoroughly knowledgeable and competent in their duties

12. No two parcels of real estate are identical. Therefore all real estate parcels are heterogeneous (unique).

13. Neighborhoods can be made up of properties that are similar in construction and design. Such neighborhoods are said to be homogeneous.

Property Ownership and Interests

1. Real property consists of land and everything attached to the land, including things that grow naturally without requiring planting and cultivation.

2. Annual crops that require planting and cultivation are personal property and are called emblements.

3. Ownership in land includes the surface of the earth, everything permanently attached to the surface, and the area above and below the surface, all of which can be owned separately.

4. A fixture is formerly personal property that has become attached to real property and thus is now a part of the real property.

5. Trade fixtures are items of personal property used in business that even if attached do not become real estate.

6. The allodial system of real property ownership used in the United States provides for private ownership of real estate.

7. Estates in land are divided into two groups: freehold estates and estates of less than freehold (nonfreeholds or leaseholds).

8. Freehold estates are fee simple estates, which are inheritable, and life estates, which are not inheritable.

9. The greatest form of ownership in real property is fee simple absolute.

10. Life estates may be in reversion or in remainder.

11. The duration of a life estate may be measured by the life tenant or by the life of another.

12. Conventional life estates are those created by someone's intentional act. Legal or statutory life estates are created by operation of law (for example, dower rights).

13. A life tenant has the right of alienation, the right of encumbrance, the right of possession and enjoyment of the property, and the right to derive certain income from it.

14. The less than freehold estates (also called leasehold estates or nonfreeholds) are estates of limited duration, providing possession and control but not title as in the case of freehold estates.

15. Leasehold estates are estate for years, estate from year to year (periodic tenancy) estate at will, and estate at sufferance.

16. Title held in the name of one person only is called ownership in severalty.

17. Michigan's Dormant Minerals Act requires recording of ownership every 20 years if minerals are owned by someone other than the property owner.

18. Joint tenancy and tenancy by the entirety include the right of survivorship and require the unities of time, title, interest, and possession.

19. Tenancy by the entirety is restricted to husband and wife and adds the fifth unity of marriage (unity of person).

20. The owner of a condominium unit holds title to the unit either in severalty or as co-owner with another, as well as title to the common areas as tenant in common with the other unit owners.

21. Creating a condominium requires recording a declaration (also called master deed), articles of association, and bylaws.

22. The Michigan Condominium Act requires that the master deed, bylaws, subdivision plans, purchase and escrow agreements, The Condominium Buyer's Handbook, and disclosure statement be given to a purchaser nine business days before the purchase agreement is binding.

23. Site condominiums could be composed of vacant land only with the Purchasers being able to build their own units.

24. A cooperative requires stock ownership in a corporation that owns a building containing cooperative apartments. Stockholders occupy apartments under a proprietary lease.

25. Interval ownership of land is called timesharing.

26. Business entities may receive, hold, and convey title to real property.

27. Michigan's Uniform Securities Act requires that people who deal with brokering, or servicing mortgages be registered with the Corporation and Securities Bureau.

Michigan Real Estate License Laws and Rules

1. License laws are an exercise of the police power of a the state,. and the purpose of these laws is to protect the public.

2. Michigan requires that people be licensed to engage in the real estate profession, although license requirements allow certain exemptions.

3. A broker is a person or an organization who, that, for consideration or a promise of consideration, performs or offers to perform aspects of real estate transactions for others.

4. A salesperson is one who performs acts that a broker is authorized to perform, but the salesperson does so on behalf of a the broker with whom he or she is associated.

5. The Department of Consumer and Industry Services Labor and Economic Growth is responsible for enforcing license laws in Michigan.

6. License laws establish standards of conduct for licensees.

7. The Department of Consumer and Industry Services Labor and Economic Growth is empowered to issue and revoke, suspend, deny, limit, or renew licenses.

8. License law requires a licensee to possess the necessary knowledge, skill, and a reputation for honest and fair dealing and ethical conduct to enter the real estate profession. Michigan License law is referred to as the Occupational Code, Act 299

9. The code incorporates the laws that pertain to all licensees in the state of Michigan, whatever the category of the license. This includes barbers, accountants, marriage counselors, and real estate licensees among others.

10. The first six articles of the code apply to all license categories. The remainder remaining articles are is assigned to a each particular license category. For example, Article 24 is the Contractors/Builders law; Article 26 is the Appraisal Law.

11. The Michigan real estate governing board, the Board of Real Estate Brokers and Salespersons, is authorized (along with the Department of Consumer and Industry Services) to promulgate rules for the real estate profession in Michigan. The rules are designed to give practitioners a guide on how to follow the law and a set of minimum standards of acceptable practice.

12. The Law applies to every citizen in the state; the rules are for practitioners only. Therefore, the general public cannot be found in violation of the rules. A practitioner may be found in violation of either both the law or and the rules.

13. Although a member of the public may file a complaint, only the Department or the Attorney General may file a formal complaint. The general public is defined as any individual residing in this state that who is the age of 18 years of age or older.

14. The Board of Real Estate Brokers and Salespersons is composed of nine members. Six belong to are from the regulated occupation, and three are from members of the general public.

15. The board is created within the department. The board's duties include:
    a. Interpreting licensure requirements
    b. Furnishing aid in investigations
    c. Attending informal conferences at the board's discretion
    d. Assisting the department in implementing this act

16. The board is charged with putting rules into operation (promulgating) that set minimal standards of acceptable practice within the real estate profession.

17. The board assesses penalties after a contested case hearing is completed.

18. Immediately upon receipt of a complaint, the department must begin an investigation of the allegations and open a correspondence file.

19. If the investigation does not show a violation, the department will close the case and forward the reasons to the complainant and to the respondent. The complainant has the right to provide additional information to reopen the case.

20. If the report shows evidence of a violation, the department or the Department of the Attorney General may prepare any of the following actions:
    a. A formal complaint
    b. A cease and desist order
    c. A notice of summary suspension

    d.   A citation

21.   A person cannot act in a capacity that requires a license without first possessing that license. Likewise, a person cannot operate a school of real estate, cosmetology, or a barber school without first being licensed. Doing either is a misdemeanor. The penalty for a first offense is $500 and/or imprisonment for 90 days. The penalty for subsequent violations is $1,000 and/or imprisonment for one year. An investigation may be conducted to enforce this law.

22.   The penalties that can be assessed for violating this law include one or more of the following:
    a.   Placement of a limitation on a license
    b.   Suspension
    c.   Denial of license
    d.   Revocation of license
    e.   A civil fine not to exceed $10,000
    f.   Censure
    g.   Probation
    h.   Restitution

23.   Licensees may be subject to any of the penalties if they do one or more of the following:
    a.   Practice fraud or deceit in obtaining a license
    b.   Practice fraud or deceit in the occupation
    c.   Violate a rule of conduct
    d.   Demonstrate a lack of good moral character
    e.   Commit an act of gross negligence
    f.   Practice false advertising
    g.   Demonstrate incompetence
    h.   Fail to comply with a subpoena, a citation, or a final order
    i.   Violate any other provision of this Act or Rule for which a penalty is
    j.   not otherwise prescribed

24.   Property management means the marketing, maintenance, and administration of real property for others for a fee, commission, compensation, or other valuable consideration, pursuant to a property management employment contract.

25.   Property management account means an interest-bearing or non interest-bearing account or instrument used in the operation of property management.

26.   A property management employment contract means is the written agreement entered into between a broker and client concerning the broker's employment as a property manager for the client, setting forth the broker's duties, responsibilities, and activities as a property manager, and setting forth the handling, management,

safekeeping, investment, disbursement and use of property management money, funds, and accounts.

27. A real estate broker can be a human being or a non-person (partnership, association, corporation, common law trust, or combination). The intent to receive a fee, compensation, or valuable consideration includes any goods or services based on money. Under license law, the following activities require a license if anything of value is rendered by others:

    a. Selling or offering for sale
    b. Buying or offering to buy
    c. Providing or offering to provide a market analysis
    d. Listing, offering, or attempting to list
    e. Negotiating the purchase, sale, exchange or mortgage of real estate (that is, engaging in any activity not regulated by the Michigan Mortgage Brokers, Lenders, and Servicers Act, P.A. 173 of 1987)
    f. Negotiating for the construction of a building on real estate
    g. Leasing or offering for rent for others (owners may lease their own property, but if they hire someone to lease it for them, that person must be licensed)
    h. Negotiating the purchase, sale, or exchange of a business, a business opportunity or the goodwill of an existing business for others
    i. Engaging in property management
    j. A person engaged in real estate as an owner or otherwise, as a principal vocation must be licensed.

28. A real estate salesperson must be a person. There is no legal provision under in license law for a salesperson to incorporate, conduct real estate business under a corporate name, and be paid by that corporation instead of directly from by their employing broker.

29. A licensed salesperson working either full or part time may perform many of the same functions as a licensed broker while employed under a broker.

30. An independent contractor relationship must meet the following conditions:
    a. The broker and the licensee must have a written agreement stating that the licensee is not an employee for federal and state income tax purposes.
    b. Not less than 75 percent of the licensee's real estate income may come from commissions earned through the sale of real estate.

31. A real estate license is issued for a term of three (3) years.

32. The following persons are exempt from holding a real estate license:
    a. Michigan licensed builders who sell what they build (up to a quadruplex that has never been occupied)
    b. Individual owners, if not more than 5 in a 12-month period (see Rule 319).

c. Individual lessors

d. Attorneys-in-fact acting under legal power of attorney

e. Persons appointed by the court

f. Persons who render services as

    I. Attorneys-at-law

    II. Receivers

    III. Trustees in bankruptcy

    IV. Administrators

    V. Executors

    VI. Persons selling under order of the court

    VII. Trustees selling under a deed of trust

g. Persons licensed under the Michigan Mortgage Brokers, Lenders, and Servicers Licensing Act

33. The educational requirements for a broker's license include successful completion of not fewer than 90 clock hours of approved classroom courses, the subject of at least nine of the hours which must be civil rights and fair housing. These hours are in addition to the hours required for a salesperson's license.

34. Prior to taking the salesperson's exam, applicants must prove that they have successfully completed not fewer than 40 hours of classroom study in real estate principles; the subject of at least four of these which must be civil rights and fair housing.

35. A licensee shall complete not less than 18 hours of continuing education per 3 year license cycle. The minimum hours per year are: 4 of the 18 hours to be completed between January 1, 2006 and December 31, 2006. There is a minimum of is 2 of the 18 hours per year thereafter.

36. Course material for continuing education must be approved by the department prior to the course being offered. At least 2 hours of a continuing education course per calendar year must involve law, rules, and court cases regarding real estate.

37. A licensee whose license has been lapsed for fewer than three years may become re-licensed by meeting the required continuing education requirements.

38. The department will not issue a broker's license to someone who has been convicted of embezzlement or misappropriation of funds.

39. A broker must maintain a place of business in the state of Michigan. If a broker maintains more than one place of business, each office must have a license. Any

branch office in excess of 25 miles from the city limits where the main office is located must be under the direct supervision of an associate broker.

40. The department will require that all broker applicants show proof of three years of full-time experience in real estate or in a field determined by the department to be relevant and related.

41. All principals (e.g., partners, officers in a corporation, etc.) must hold an associate broker's license. An associate broker shall meet the same requirements as a broker. An associate broker's license will be issued only to individuals.

42. The license of a principal associate broker who ceases to be connected with the entity will be automatically suspended.

43. The licenses of non-principal associate brokers are transferable in the same manner as a salesperson's license.

44. If the department revokes a broker's license, the licenses of all salespersons and associate brokers in the office will be automatically suspended pending a change of employer and the issuance of new licenses.

45. A non-principal associate broker shall not have more than one license issued

46. Salespersons are prohibited from accepting a commission or valuable consideration from anyone other than their employing broker.

47. A licensee may never use a lottery, a contest, a game, a prize, or a drawing for the sale or promotion of a sale of real estate. A game promotion may be used, however, if it complies with the Michigan penal code, and is not for the direct promotion of a specific piece of real estate. The penal code defines game promotion and gives the parameters within which a game promotion may be conducted.

48. If Michigan brokers want to promote in Michigan property that is located in another state, they must comply with the Out of State Land Sales rules by:
    a. Submitting full particulars to the department
    b. Complying with all rules, restrictions, and conditions set by the department
    c. Paying all expenses incurred by the department in investigating the promotion

    The broker cannot indicate in any advertising that the property promotion was approved by the department.

49. Licensees are subject to any Article 6 penalties if they do any of the following:
    a. Act (except in a case involving property management) for more than one party in a transaction without all parties' written permission
    b. Fail to provide written agency disclosure to any prospective buyer or seller
    c. Represent someone other than the broker without the broker's consent

d. Fail to remit money to the broker that belongs to others.

e. Change home or business addresses without notifying the department

f. Fail to return a licensee's license within five days of the licensee's leaving the employment of the broker (brokers only)

g. In the case of a licensee engaged in property management, violation of Section 2512 C (2), (5), or (6)

h. Pay a fee or valuable consideration to someone not licensed, including someone who gives a licensee a referral. (A broker cannot pay any licensees except those licensed to his office but may pay a commission to an out-of-state broker if the out-of-state broker does not conduct any licensed activity in Michigan. Payment for a commercially prepared list of names is permitted.)

i. Conduct or prepare a market analysis that does not comply with the requirements mandated in the Appraisers Law. (The law states that a broker is allowed to charge a fee for a market analysis if it does not involve a federally related transaction, if the analysis is in writing, and if it states in boldface type: This is a market analysis, not an appraisal, and was prepared by a licensed real estate broker or associate broker, not a licensed appraiser.)

j. Failing to deposit monies belonging to others in an escrow account That money must remain in the account until the transaction closes or is otherwise terminated. Salespersons must turn all these monies over to their broker. A broker cannot take advance payment out of the escrow account. The time frame for money to be deposited is mandated in law as within two banking days after the broker has received notice that an offer to purchase is has been accepted by all parties.

50. Licensees who want to sue for compensation must be able to prove they were licensed at the time the compensation was earned.

51. A landlord may pay and an existing tenant may accept as much as one-half of one month's rent for referring new tenants to a complex without violating license law.

52. Property management.

a. Except as otherwise provided in this section, all property management duties, responsibilities, and activities performed by a real estate broker and his or her agent engaged in property management shall be governed by and performed in accordance with a property management employment contract.

b. A real estate broker who engages in property management shall maintain property management accounts separate from all other accounts except as provided in this section. A property management account shall be managed in accordance with the property management employment contract.

c. A property management account may be an interest-bearing account or instrument, unless the property management employment contract provides to the contrary. The interest earned on a property management account shall be handled in accordance with the property management employment contract.

d. A real estate broker or any designated employee of the real estate broker engaged in property management may be signatory on drafts or checks drawn on property management accounts.

e. A person who engages in property management shall maintain records of funds deposited and withdrawn from property management accounts. Property management account records shall indicate the date of the transaction, from whom the money was received or to whom it was given disbursed, and all other pertinent information concerning the transaction as set forth in the property management employment contract. may require.

f. A real estate broker engaged in property management shall render an accounting to his or her property management client and remit all money strictly in accordance with the property management employment contract.

53. The department may, if a license has been denied, suspended, or revoked, require the applicant to post a bond before a license is re-issued. In this event, the department can require that the bond be issued for not more than $5,000 for a period not to exceed five years.

54. Michigan does not have a residency requirement for licensees. The law states that a nonresident must meet the Michigan requirements for licensure and sign an irrevocable consent to service of process. Legally admitted resident aliens may become licensed.

55. Every listing service provision agreement must state that it is against the law to discriminate on the basis of race, color, religion, sex, national origin, age, marital status, familial status, or disability.

56. The mandatory agency disclosure law states that, prior to the disclosure of confidential information, a licensee must disclose to a potential buyer or seller all types of agency relationships available under Michigan law. The form should be filled out and signed by the licensee according to the broker's predetermined policies and procedures in order to explain the agency relationship to the potential buyer or seller. The disclosure form must substantially conform to the form outlined in the law. The signatures of the potential buyer and seller acknowledge only receipt of the information prior to the disclosure of confidential information. The disclosure form is not a contract. for agency.

57. Activities for which licensees will not be subject to disciplinary action:
a. Failure to disclose that a former occupant of a property has or is suspected of having a disability.
b. Failure to disclose that the property was or was suspected of being the site of a homicide, a suicide, or other occurrence prohibited by law that had has no material effect on the condition of the property.

c. Failure to disclose any information from the compilation that is provided or made available under through the Sex Offenders Registration Act.

58. Non-principal associate broker is an individual who is not a sole proprietor, an officer or equity owner, a member, manager, or general partner in the company.

59. Principal associate broker is an individual who is a sole proprietor, an officer or equity owner, a member, manager or general partner in the company.

60. A "service provision agreement" is an agreement between the broker and client which establishes an agency relationship.

61. Supervision is defined as overseeing of, or participation in, the work of another licensed individual by a broker or associate broker.

62. A broker's license shall be issued to a legal entity only if the individual applying is a sole proprietor, partner or limited partner.

63. An associate broker's or salesperson's license can be issued only to individuals.

64. The department defines full time as six transactions in a twelve-month period. which is one year's credit for a license.

65. Relevant and related experience may be earned toward broker's license requirements as follows:

   a. Builders who have built and sold or leased six residential, commercial, or industrial units or combination during 12 months earn a one-year credit.

   b. Investors earn a six-month credit for every six five personally negotiated transactions with a total credit allowed of one year. Negotiating more than five transactions constitutes unlicensed activity [see Rule 359.23319(i)(a)] and so no credit is shall be given.

   c. Land or condominium developers earn a one-year credit for every two developments of 10 units or more.

   d. Attorneys must who have acted as an attorney for six real estate transactions per 12-month period.

   e. A person who works a 40-hour week in a 48-week year and is in a decision-making capacity in a field related to real estate (loan or trust officer, title insurance officer, appraiser) may receive a one-year credit for each year of meeting these criteria.

A person who is in an occupation that requires a license must possess that license to receive relevant and related experience credit.

66. Examination scores are valid for one year from the date the exam was taken and passed.

67. A salesperson or non-principal associate broker who wants to transfer his or her license after it is issued must:
    a. Submit a transfer form to the department with the proper fees.
    b. Have his or her pocket card signed and dated by new broker.

68. A broker must advertise in the name under which the license is issued.

69. Every service provision agreement must be completely filled out prior to the client signing it. The client must receive a true copy at the time of signing. All service provision agreements must have a definite expiration date. A service provision agreement shall not contain a provision requiring the client to notify the broker of the client's intention to cancel the listing upon or after the expiration date. No automatic renewal clause is allowed in any service provision agreement.

70. A purchaser must receive a copy of an offer to purchase immediately upon signing it. A licensee must promptly deliver all offers to the seller. Acceptable methods of delivery include but are not limited to either of the following:
    a. delivery in person or by mail
    b. delivery by electronic communication. The use of electronic records or digital signatures for any real estate transaction requires the prior agreement of the parties
    The seller must receive a copy at the time of signing and the purchaser must receive a copy showing the seller's signature.

71. A broker or associate broker must supervise the work of a licensee. Supervision shall include, at a minimum, direct communication in person, or by radio, telephone, or electronic communication on a regular basis; review the practices and reports of the supervised individual; analysis and guidance of the licensee's performance; providing written operating policies and procedures.

72. The broker involved in the a closing must furnish or cause to be furnished to the buyer and to the seller a complete and detailed closing statement showing all receipts and disbursements of the transaction. The broker may provide separate statements to the buyer and to the seller.

    Salespersons cannot close a real estate transaction except under the direct supervision of their broker. The broker must sign the final closing document. The closing statement must reflect the agreement between the buyer and the seller. The broker cannot change or alter the purchase agreement without the written permission of all parties to the transaction. A licensee may not close a transaction that is contrary to the terms spelled out in the executed agreement between the buyer and the seller. A broker may delegate the completion of the closing statements, but the responsibility of its accuracy and signing remains with the listing broker.

In a cooperative transaction, either broker may prepare the closing statement, but the ultimate responsibility for its figures accuracy will be with the listing broker. The listing broker must sign the final closing documents even if the transaction is closed at a bank or a title insurance company.

73.   All trust accounts must be demand accounts only. Checks must be signed by the broker or by an associate broker. Co-signatories may be used. The account must be non interest-bearing and must be maintained in accordance with license law. A broker may have more than one trust account and may have as much as $500 of personal money in each account strictly for maintenance of the account.

The minimal acceptable bookkeeping system a broker must maintain includes the following:

a.   A record that shows all money coming in and going out in chronological sequence.

Receipts must show

    I.   The date of receipt
    II.   The date of the deposit
    III.   The name of the party giving the money
    IV.   The name of the seller
    V.   The amount

Disbursements must show:

    I.   The date of the disbursement
    II.   The name of the payee
    III.   The check number
    IV.   The purpose of the disbursement
    V.   The amount of the disbursement

A current balance must be maintained.

b.   A record that shows the receipt and disbursements of each transaction.

    I.   The names of the parties to the transaction
    II.   The property address or a brief legal description
    III.   The dates and amounts received
    IV.   The date of the disbursements
    V.   The payee
    VI.   The check number
    VII.   The amount of the disbursement

74. A licensee buying or acquiring interest in property must be able to prove that he disclosed his licensure in writing to the seller prior to the seller signing the offer to purchase.

75. A licensee shall not be party to a net service provision agreement

76. If a licensee is buying or acquiring property, either directly or indirectly a commission, fee, or valuable consideration cannot be charged collected by the licensee without the prior, written consent of the seller.

77. Principal vocation is defined as:

   a. Engaging in more than five real estate sales in any 12-month period
   b. Presenting oneself to the public as being principally engaged in real estate
   c. Devoting more than 50 percent of one's working time or 15 hours per week in any six-month period to the sale of real estate

78. The only property a salesperson may sell "by owner" is his principal residence. All other licensee-owned properties must be sold through a licensed real estate broker.

79. A licensee cannot accept kickbacks, rebates, or placement fees from any parties without the prior written consent of the purchasers and the sellers in a transaction.

80. A broker cannot have a contract with a licensee that indicates that the broker does not have the responsibility to supervise the licensee.

81. All advertisements by a real estate broker must include the broker's name and telephone number or address. A broker may advertise in his own name if the property is personally owned, property, provided he identifies himself as a licensed broker in the advertisements. All other advertising must be under the direct supervision and in the name of the employing broker. The only property a salesperson can advertise for sale in his own name is his principal residence and personally owned property for rent.

82. An authorized representative of the department has the authority to enter a broker's place of business and ask for and receive any and all documents pertaining to an investigation or audit of any licensee in that office.

Agency

1. Agency is usually created with an agreement but also can be implied by the agent's conduct. A fiduciary relationship exists between every principal and their agent in an agency relationship.

2. Agencies are classified as universal, general, and special.

3. The classification of agency depends on the scope of authority given to the agent by the principal.

4. The types of real estate agency relationships are seller agency, buyer agency, and dual agency.

5. Transaction coordinators do not represent the buyers or the sellers.

6. Compensation does not determine agency. The seller, buyer, or a third party may pay the commission.

7. A multiple listing service (MLS) offers cooperation and compensation to participating members.

8. Fiduciary responsibilities of the agent include confidentiality, loyalty, obedience, reasonable skill and care, disclosure, and accounting.

9. The agent has the responsibility to deal fairly and honestly with all customers.

10. The principal has a common law duty of disclosure and fairness to all parties.

11. Michigan has a mandatory agency disclosure law for one-to-four-family residential transactions. It requires agents to disclose whom they represent prior to the customer/client disclosing any confidential information.

12. A recent change to the Michigan Agency Disclosure law requires agents to disclose the 5 minimum services they must perform under seller agency. They are:
    a. Marketing of the client's property in the manner agreed upon in the agreement
    b. Acceptance and presentation of offers and counteroffers to buy, sell or lease the client's property
    c. Assistance in developing, communicating, negotiating, and presenting offers, counteroffers, and related notices or documents until a purchase or lease agreement is executed by all parties and all contingencies are satisfied or waived
    d. After execution of a purchase agreement, assistance as necessary to complete the transaction under the terms specified in the purchase agreement
    e. Furnishing, or causing to be furnished, a complete and detailed settlement statement

13. Michigan's Seller Disclosure Act requires all one-to four-family residential sellers to complete and provide to a buyer a mandated form disclosing what they know about the property.

14.   Designated agency allows a company to designate an agent as the seller's representative and another to represent the buyer. If a buyer under contract wishes to purchase a company's listing, the Broker is a dual agent for this in-house transaction.

15.   The Michigan Antitrust Act prohibits certain activities known as trade restraints by licensees including territorial agreements, boycotts, tying agreements and leading the public to believe that fees and services are not negotiable.

Fair Housing

1.   The Civil Rights Act of 1968, as amended, prohibits discrimination in housing due to a party's race, color, religion, sex, national origin, age, disability, or familial status. Disability and familial status were added in 1988.

2.   Discrimination is prohibited in (a) sale or rental of housing, (b) advertising the sale or rental of housing, (c) financing of housing, and (d) provision of real estate brokerage services. The act also makes blockbusting, steering, and redlining illegal.

3.   Four exemptions are provided to owners in selling or renting housing: (a) owners who do not own more than three houses, (b) owners of apartment buildings with not more than four apartments when the owner occupies one of the apartments, (c) religious organizations, as to properties used for the benefit of members only, and (d) private clubs, as to lodging used for the benefit of members only. The owners' exemptions are not available if the owner used discriminatory advertising or the services of a real estate broker.

4.   Enforcement of Title VIII of the 1968 Civil Rights Act was amended significantly in 1988. Enforcement procedures now include (a) administrative procedure through the Office of Equal Opportunity of HUD, which first attempts voluntary conciliation and then can refer the case to an administrative law judge, who can impose financial penalties of $10,000 to $50,000; (b) civil suit in federal court; and (c) action by the U. S. Attorney General, who may file a suit in federal court and impose penalties of up to $50,000 on the first offense in a "pattern of discrimination."

5.   The Civil Rights Act of 1866 prohibits discrimination only on the basis of race. The prohibition is not limited to housing but includes all real estate transactions. The act may be enforced only by civil suit in federal court. This law has no exemptions.

6.   Michigan has passed its own civil rights acts (The Elliott–Larsen Civil Rights Act) that virtually duplicates the federal law, with two added protected classes, age and marital status. Michigan state law is substantially equivalent to the federal law.

Complaints filed with HUD will be referred to the state agency for investigation and enforcement.

7. The Americans with Disabilities Act provides that individuals with disabilities cannot be denied access to public transportation, any commercial facility, or public accommodation. Barriers in existing buildings must be removed if readily achievable. New buildings must be readily accessible and usable by individuals with disabilities.

Contract Law

1. A contract is an agreement between legally competent parties, with consideration, to do or to abstain from doing some legal act.

2. An express contract is spoken or written. An implied contract is one inferred from the actions of the parties.

3. Bilateral contracts are based on mutual promises. Unilateral contracts are based on a promise by one party and an act by another party.

4. An executed contract has been signed or fully performed. An executory contract has provisions yet to be performed.

5. A contract is created by the unconditional acceptance of a valid offer. Acceptance of bilateral offers must be communicated. Communication of the acceptance of unilateral offers results from the performance of an act by the optionee.

6. Contracts that have an illegal purpose or are missing an essential element are void.

7. A voidable contract is one that may not be enforceable at the option of one of the parties to the contract.

8. The requirements for contract validity are:
   a. competent parties
   b. reality of consent
   c. offer and acceptance
   d. consideration
   e. legality of object, and
   f. possibility to complete

9. An offer must not be indefinite or illusory.

10. An offeror may revoke an offer at any time prior to acceptance.

11. Consideration is anything of value, including a promise.

12. Reality of consent is defeated and a contract made voidable by:
    a. misrepresentation,
    b. fraud,
    c. undue influence,
    d. duress, or
    e. mutual mistake.

13. Contracts are assignable in the absence of a specific prohibition against assignment within the contract.

14. The remedies for breach of contract are
    a. compensatory damages,
    b. liquidated damages,
    c. specific performance, and
    d. rescission.

15. If a contracting party defaults in the performance of contractual obligations, the injured party may sue for damages in a suit for breach of contract. If the contract is for the purchase and sale of real property, an alternative remedy in the form of a lawsuit for specific performance is available to the injured party.

16. The Michigan Uniform Vendor and Purchasers Risk Act is designed to protect the purchaser in the event the property is destroyed prior to closing.

17. A land contract is also called a contract for deed, a conditional sales contract, or an installment land contract. It is a contract of sale and a method of financing by the seller for the buyer. Legal title does not pass until the buyer pays all or some specified part of the purchase price. The contract buyer holds an interest referred to as equitable title until the transfer of legal title.

18. The Doctrine of Equitable Conversion states that the vendor cannot do anything to jeopardize the equitable interest of the vendee.

19. An option provides a right to purchase property under specified terms and conditions. During the option term, the contract is binding on the optionor but not on the optionee. When an option is exercised, it becomes a contract of sale and is, therefore, binding on both parties.

Transfers of Title

1. Transfer of title is termed alienation. Involuntary alienation occurs during life as a result of adverse possession, lien foreclosure sale, or condemnation under the power of eminent domain. Involuntary alienation after death is escheat. Voluntary alienation after death is by will or descent. Voluntary alienation during life can occur only by delivery of a valid deed.

2. The requirements for deed validity in Michigan are (1) must be in writing, (2) competent grantor, (3) competent or incompetent grantee, (4) grantor and grantee named with certainty, (5) adequate legal property description, (6) recital of consideration, (7) words of conveyance, (8) habendum clause, (9) proper execution by grantor, and (10) delivery and acceptance to convey title.

3. To be eligible for recording on the public record, a deed must be acknowledged. Recording protects the grantee's title against creditors of the grantor and subsequent conveyances by the grantor.

4. A general warranty deed is the strongest and broadest form of title guarantee. The general warranty deed typically contains five covenants: The covenant of seisin and right to convey; The covenant against encumbrances; The covenant of quiet enjoyment; The covenant of further assurances; and The covenant of warranty of title.

5. A quitclaim deed is a deed of release and contains no warranties. It will convey whatever interest the grantor may have. The quitclaim deed is used mainly to remove a cloud from a title or to release dower, a lien or other interest.

6. The purpose of a title examination is to determine the quality of a title. The examination must be made by an attorney or a title insurance company. Only an attorney can legally give an opinion as to the quality of a title.

7. A title insurance policy protects the insured against financial loss caused due to a title defect.

8. Revenue stamps in Michigan are $8.60 per $1,000 based on the sales price of the property ($4.30 per $500). It is rounded up to the next $500.

9. $1.10 per $1,000 of revenue stamps goes to the county. $7.50 per $1,000 goes to the state.

10. The three methods of property description in use in the United States are metes and bounds, reference, and rectangular survey.

11. Metes and bounds are measurements and boundaries. It is the most exact method of property description.

12. Reference or lot and block is a legally sufficient method of property description.

13. Rectangular survey method involves the principal meridian and baseline, the tier (township) and range lines, and the townships of a state grid.

14. A township is 6 x 6 miles square or 36 square miles. Each section within a township is one mile square (640 acres).

15. There are 43,560 square feet in an acre.

Real Estate Finance

1. The purpose of a mortgage or deed of trust (trust deed) is to secure the payment of the promissory note.

2. A promissory note is a contract in which the borrower promises to pay back the money borrowed and specifies the manner in which it will be paid.

3. A fully amortizing mortgage requires payments of principal and interest that will retire the debt completely over the mortgage term.

4. A mortgage is a two-party instrument. A deed of trust is a three-party instrument.

5. The requirements for mortgage or deed of trust validity are (1) it must be in writing, (2) it must be between competent parties, (3) there must be evidence of a valid debt (the note), (4) the mortgagor must have a valid interest in the property being mortgaged, (5) it must contain a legally acceptable property description, (6) it must have a mortgaging clause, (7) there must be a defeasance clause allowing for removal of the lien upon full payment of the debt, (8) execution by borrower (only the borrower signs), and (9) delivery to and acceptance by lender.

6. The borrower's rights are (1) possession of the property prior to default, (2) defeat of the lien by paying the debt in full prior to default, (3) equitable redemption, and (4) statutory redemption.

7. The lender's rights are (1) possession of the property upon default, (2) foreclosure, and (3) right to assign the mortgage.

8.	The two categories of foreclosure are judicial and non-judicial. After the cost of the sale are paid, foreclosure sale proceeds are distributed in order of priority, based upon the time and date of recording. If the sale proceeds available to the lender are insufficient to satisfy the debt, the lender may sue for a deficiency judgment.

9.	A buyer assuming a seller's mortgage assumes liability on both the mortgage and the note. The seller remains liable on the note unless specifically released by a mortgage clause or by the lender. A buyer taking title subject to an existing mortgage has no liability on the note.

10.	The Michigan Due on Sale Clause Act applies only to state-chartered lenders.

11.	The major sources of residential financing are savings banks, mutual savings banks, commercial banks, and mortgage bankers. Of these, savings banks have traditionally provided more funds for the purchase, construction and improvement of one to four family housing than any other single source, though the gap between savings institutions and commercial banks narrowed significantly after the S & L shake-up in the 1980s. When all types of mortgages (residential, commercial, and farm) are considered, commercial banks hold more mortgage loans than do savings institutions.

12.	The primary mortgage market consists of lending institutions making loans directly to individual borrowers. The secondary mortgage market provides for the purchase of existing mortgages between lenders and the sale of mortgages by lenders to Fannie Mae (FNMA), Ginnie Mae (GNMA), and Freddie Mac (FHLMC). The secondary market provides liquidity to mortgages, thereby reducing the effect of disintermediation for the benefit of lending institutions and borrowers as well.

13.	The Michigan Mortgage Brokers, Lenders and Servicers Licensing Act requires separate licensing for anyone acting in any of these three categories.

14.	Methods of financing include insured and uninsured conventional mortgage loans, FHA-insured loans, VA-guaranteed loans, and the various types of seller financing.

15.	Conventional loans are not required to be insured if the loan amount does not exceed 80 percent the sale price of the property, also known as the loan-to-value ratio (LTV). Most conventional insured loans are 90 percent and 95 percent LTV. This insurance is known as private mortgage insurance (PMI). The premium is paid by the borrower.

16.	Various types of mortgages include junior, term, amortizing, balloon, open-end, graduated payment, adjustable or variable rate, reverse annuity mortgage (RAM), shared appreciation (SAM), growing equity (GEM), participation, wraparound, package, blanket, construction, purchase money, and leasehold mortgages.

17. FHA-insured and VA-guaranteed loans are made by specifically qualified lending institutions.

18. FHA insurance, called mortgage insurance premium (MIP), protects the lender from financial loss in the event of foreclosure. The borrower pays the premium. FHA establishes a maximum loan amount.

19. VA loans are guaranteed loans. The current guarantee is a multi-tiered system. VA loans may be made for up to 100 percent of the sales price or the property value established by a VA appraisal and stated in the Certificate of Reasonable Value (CRV) issued by the VA, whichever is less.

20. FHA-insured and VA-guaranteed loans require escrow accounts and are for 30-year terms or shorter. Both are assumable with certain restrictions and do not impose a prepayment penalty. The down payment can be borrowed if it is secured by collateral.

21. Borrowers may pay points in an FHA, VA or a conventional loan to buy down the rate or when otherwise required.

22. The Rural Housing Service (RHS) direct loan program provides a number of homeownership opportunities to rural Americans whose income is below median income levels for the area.

23. Federal laws that regulate lending institutions in making consumer loans include Regulation Z, part of the Truth in Lending Simplification and Reform Act (TILSRA), the Real Estate Settlement Procedures Act (RESPA), and the Equal Credit Opportunity Act (ECOA).

24. State of Michigan usury laws set the maximum rate of interest for private parties and other unregulated lenders at 11 percent.

25. Real estate agents in Michigan are liable under Michigan's Consumer Protection Act.

Real Estate Appraisal

1. Real estate licensees who perform market analyses are exempt from having an appraisal license according to Michigan Appraisal Law.

2. An appraisal is an estimate (not a determination) of value based upon factual data at a particular time for a particular purpose on a particular property.

3. Market value is the amount of money a typical buyer will give in exchange for a property.

4. The various types of value include market value, assessed value, insurance value, mortgage loan value, condemnation value, and book value.

5. Property value is dependent upon effective demand, utility, scarcity and transferability (DUST).

6. The basic valuation principles are highest and best use, substitution, supply and demand, conformity, anticipation, contribution, increasing or diminishing returns, competition, change, depreciation and age.

7. Depreciation is the loss in value from any cause. In structures, the causes of depreciation are (a) physical deterioration, (b) functional obsolescence, and (c) economic obsolescence.

8. The market data or comparison approach to value is the most appropriate appraisal method for estimating the value of single-family, owner-occupied dwellings and vacant land.

9. The income approach, or appraisal by capitalization, is the most appropriate appraisal method for estimating the value of property that produces rental income. The capitalization formula is:

VALUE X CAPITALIZATION RATE = NET OPERATING INCOME

10. A gross rent multiplier may be appropriate for estimating the value of rental property. It is a simplified version of the capitalization formula.

11. The cost approach is the main appraisal method for estimating the value of property that does not fall into the other categories. These properties, known as special-use properties, include museums, hospitals, schools, and churches, as well as new construction.

12. An appraisal report provides a value estimate based upon a correlation of the estimates obtained by all three appraisal approaches.

Land Use Controls

1. The plan for development is enforced by zoning ordinances. Planning and zoning are exercises of police power.

2. Types of zones include residential, commercial, planned unit developments (PUDs), industrial, and agricultural.

3. Zoning may be either exclusive-use or cumulative-use.

4. In addition to specifying permitted uses, zoning ordinances define standards and requirements that must be met for each type of usage.

5. A nonconforming use is one that differs from the type of use permitted in a certain zone. The nonconforming use may be lawful or unlawful.

6. A variance is a deviation from specific requirements of a zoning ordinance which is permitted because the property owner would be subject to a special hardship imposed by strict enforcement.

7. Spot zoning occurs when a certain property within a zoned area is rezoned to permit a use that is different from the zoning requirements for that area. Spot zoning may be valid or invalid.

8. Exclusionary zoning imposes zoning restrictions that could be considered discriminatory.

9. The purpose of planning is to provide for the orderly growth of a community that will result in the greatest social and economic benefits to the property owners.

10. Subdivision ordinances regulate the development of residential subdivisions. These ordinances protect property purchasers as well as taxpayers in the area from increased tax burdens in providing essential services to the subdivisions. Michigan's Land Division Act details the orderly layout of land. It states that once a parcel is split, it cannot be split again for ten years.

11. Building codes require certain standards of construction. The codes are concerned primarily with electrical and plumbing systems, fire and safety standards, and sanitary systems and equipment.

12. The Interstate Land Sales Full Disclosure Act regulates sale of unimproved lots in interstate commerce to prevent fraudulent schemes in selling land sight unseen.

13. Many areas of Michigan have mandatory city certification on the transfer of real estate.

14. The Michigan Land Sales Act exempts certain land promotions from disclosure requirements.

15. Michigan out-of-state Land Sales requires that out-of-state land be promoted in Michigan by a Michigan licensed broker who must: (a) submit all particulars to the

department; (b) pay up to $500 for transportation plus all on site inspection fees; (c) not advertise that the promotion is approved; and (d) give the buyer a property report prior to the signing of an offer to purchase.

16. Federal environmental laws include: (a) Comprehensive Environmental Response, Compensation, and Liability Act (CERCLA; (b) Superfund Amendments and Reauthorization Act (SARA); (c) Underground Storage Tanks (UST); (d) Resource Conservation and Recovery Act (RCRA); (e) Clean Water Act (CWA); (f) Clean Air Act (CAA); and (g) Toxic Substances Control Act (TSCA), all of which are designed to protect the environment.

17. Radon is an odorless, colorless gas that could cause lung cancer.

18. The Federal Lead-based Paint Disclosure Act requires disclosure by sellers or landlords of the existence of lead-based paint in properties for sale or lease that were built prior to 1978. It also requires renovators to make certain disclosures prior to beginning a renovation.

19. The Michigan Environmental Protection Act, like the federal laws, requires disclosure and provides for the protection of the environment. It also assigns responsibility for cleanup to the parties responsible for the contamination.

20. Brownfield redevelopment in Michigan allows for once contaminated land to be put back into use by providing assistance in demolition, infrastructure development and tax credits.

21. Michigan Right to Farm Act protects farmers from litigation for being a nuisance if they follow established guidelines.

22. Michigan's Wetland Protection Act allows cities to regulate and preserve wetlands by ordinances that are more restrictive than state law.

23. Private land use controls are in the form of deed restrictions and subdivision restrictive covenants.

24. Restrictive covenants must be reasonable and must be equally beneficial to all property owners.

25. Restrictive covenants are recorded on the public record in an instrument called a declaration of restrictions. These covenants are not legally effective and enforceable unless they are recorded.

26. Restrictive covenants are enforced by court injunction upon petition by the property

owners on a timely basis.

Encumbrances and Government Restrictions

1   Encumbrance is a claim, lien, charge, or liability attached to and binding upon real property. Examples are encroachments, easements, liens, assessments, and restrictive covenants.

2.   Easements are non-possessory interests in land owned by another. Easements can be in gross or appurtenant in nature. Easements are created by grant, necessity, prescription, implication, and condemnation.

3.   Specific liens are claims against a specific and readily identifiable property, such as a mortgage or real estate taxes.

4.   General liens are claims against a person and all of his or her property, such as a judgment resulting from a lawsuit.

5.   The lien for real property taxes is a specific lien and is given first priority in Michigan.

6.   Real property taxation is on an ad valorem (by value) basis.

7.   Michigan property tax is based on the total value of the land and the buildings. The assessed value is usually 50 percent of the market value.

8.   The Michigan Construction Lien Act requires that a Notice of Commencement, Notice of Furnishing, Sworn Statement, and Waiver of Lien be used on all construction projects.

9.   The property of a debtor is subject to a forced sale to satisfy an unpaid judgment.

10.   A lis pendens notice provides specific and constructive notice to the public that a lawsuit concerning certain real estate is pending.

12.   Restrictive covenants are used to preserve the quality of land and maximize land values.

13.   An encroachment is a trespass on land, an intrusion or breaking over the boundary of land.

14.   Proof of the existence or lack of existence of an encroachment is evidenced by a survey of the boundary.

36

15. Private ownership of property is subject to the four powers of government.: Eminent domain, police power (such as zoning, health, and building codes), taxation, and escheat.

16. A profit in real property is transferable and inheritable. A license or bailment in real property is not transferable or inheritable.

17. Inherent ownership rights include air rights, mineral rights, riparian, and littoral water rights.

18. Michigan's Dormant Minerals Act requires re-recording an interest in mineral rights every 20 years if the mineral rights are owned by someone other than the property owner.

Leasehold Estates

1. A lease is a contract between the owner of property and the tenant. The landlord or owner is the lessor; the tenant is the lessee.

2. The landlord and tenant are bound by contractual rights and obligations created by the lease agreement.

3. Landlords and tenants should thoroughly understand the Michigan Truth in Renting Act and Michigan Security Deposits Act.

4. The transfer of the entire remaining term of a lease by the lessee is an assignment. A transfer of part of the lease term with a reversion to the lessee is a subletting.

5. In a lease of residential property, the landlord has the duty to keep the premises habitable for the tenant.

6. The tenant has a duty to maintain and return the premises to the landlord, at expiration of the lease, in the same condition it was in at the beginning of the lease, ordinary wear and tear excepted.

7. The tenant can make a claim of constructive eviction when the premises becomes uninhabitable because of the landlord's lack of maintenance. A claim of constructive eviction will terminate the lease.

8. Leases are terminated by (a) expiration of lease term, (b) mutual agreement, (c) breach of condition (d) eviction or (f) constructive eviction.

9.   Leases are nonfreehold estates.

10.   The two main classifications of leases are gross lease and net lease. In a gross lease, the landlord pays the real property taxes, insurance, and maintenance of the property. In a net lease, the tenant pays all or some portion of these expenses in addition to a flat monthly rental payment.

11.   Types of lease include the graduated lease, escalated lease, index lease, fixed lease, reappraisal lease, percentage lease, ground lease, oil and gas leases, and sale and leaseback

Property Management

1.   Property managers are agents engaged in the management of property for others, for a fee and, therefore, must have a real estate license.

2.   The management agreement is a contract in which a property owner employs a property manager to act as his or her agent.

3.   The property manager's basic responsibilities are (a) to produce the highest possible net operating income from the property and (b) to maintain and increase the value of the principal's investment.

4.   Properties that may require management are condominiums, cooperatives, apartments, single-family rental houses, mobile home parks, office buildings, shopping malls, and industrial property.

5.   Property managers fulfill their basic responsibilities by formulating a management plan, soliciting tenants, leasing space, collecting rent, hiring and training employees, maintaining good tenant relations, providing for preventative and corrective maintenance, protecting tenants, maintaining adequate insurance, keeping adequate records, and auditing and paying bills.

6.   The property management report is a periodic accounting provided by a property manager to the property owner.

7.   A fire insurance policy indemnifies the insured against loss by fire. Protection from losses by other hazards may be obtained by an extended coverage endorsement.

8.   Package policies, called homeowner's policies, provide all the usual protections in one policy. These policies are available to both homeowners and renters.

9. To be eligible for insurance, the applicant must have an insurable interest in the property, such as buyer and seller in a contract, owner, part owner, trustee, receiver, tenant, mortgagor or mortgagee.

10. Every hazard insurance policy contains a coinsurance clause requiring the owner to insure the property for at least 80 percent of the property value to recover up to the face amount of the policy in the event of a partial loss. If the loss equals or exceeds the amount of coverage required by the coinsurance clause, however, the insurance company will pay the policy amount even though the requirement of the coinsurance clause is not met.

11. Insurance policies usually are assignable with the written consent of the insurance company. The consent is evidenced by an endorsement to the policy.

12. Homeowner's warranty policies are available to purchasers of newly constructed and existing houses. These policies insure against many, but not all, structural and mechanical defects.

Taxation

1. Real estate licensees should be knowledgeable about tax legislation but should encourage clients to seek professional tax advice when necessary.

2. The Tax Reform Act of 1986 and Revenue Reconciliation Act of 1993 reduced capital gains benefits and lengthened depreciation schedules for investment property.

3. Depreciation is a deductible allowance from net income in arriving at taxable income. Therefore, it provides a tax shelter for the property owner.

4. A homeowner's real estate property taxes and mortgage interest, subject to certain limits, are deductible expenses in calculating federal income tax.

5. Losses incurred in the sale of a personal residence are not tax deductible.

6. The Taxpayer Relief Act of 1997 allows an exclusion from taxation of up to $500,000 in capital gain for married homeowners and up to $250,000 for single homeowners on the sale of a principal residence.

7. The 1997 law allows the exclusion to be used if the owner occupied the property for 2 of the last 5 years prior to the sale.

8. Homeowners essentially can take advantage of the capital gains exclusion under the 1997 law every two years provided the property has been occupied as a principal residence.

9. First-time homebuyers (someone who has not owned a home within the two-year period ending on the date of acquisition of a principal residence) are allowed to withdraw up to $10,000 from a retirement plan to use for the purchase of a home without penalty. This incentive also applies if the money is withdrawn from the retirement account of a spouse, parent, grandparent, or certain other relatives.

10. Depreciation enables the owner of business or investment property to recover the cost or other basis of the asset.

11. Land is not depreciable. Only structures and improvements on the land are depreciable real property.

12. When a depreciable asset is sold, the basis of the asset used to compute taxable gain is the depreciated value, not the price the seller pays for the property.

13. Expenses of operating business or investment property are deductible expenses in arriving at taxable income.

14. To qualify as a tax-deferred exchange, like-kind property must be exchanged. An exchanger receiving cash (boot) or other unlike-kind property in addition to like-kind property is taxed on the value of the boot or other unlike-kind property received.

15. To qualify as a tax-deferred exchange, the property exchanged must have been held for use in business (other than inventory) or as an investment. Property held for personal use does not qualify.

16. Investment analysis requires careful attention to tax consequences as well as cash flow analysis.

Introduction to Real Estate Principles

1. The greater the supply of any commodity in comparison to demand, the

A. higher the value will be.
B. more demand there will be.
C. less demand there will be.
D. lower the value will be.

2. The real estate market is an excellent example of which market concept?

A. Closed market
B. Free market
C. Slow market
D. Fast market

3. Of the following characteristics, which has the greatest effect on property value?

A. Permanence of improvement
B. Location
C. Indestructibility
D. Immobility

4. All of the following are attributes of real property EXCEPT

A. surface of the land.
B. air space above the land.
C. minerals beneath the surface.
D. items that are not attached to the land.

5. The use of land that best preserves its utility, provides the greatest income, and results in its greatest present value is

A. economic conditions.
B. highest and best use.
C. physical characteristics.
D. fair market value.

6. A term REALTOR® is the trade name for a member of:

A. the National Association of REALTORS®.
B. the Appraisal Foundation.
C. any real estate agency.
D. the Association of Real Estate License Law Officials (ARELLO).

7. The agreement by which a property owner employs a real estate firm to market a property is a/an

A. sales contract.
B. listing contract.
C. appraisal.
D. settlement.

8. What factors are considered in determining the highest and best use of land?

A. Financial capabilities of the investor
B. Physical and economic characteristics
C. Real and personal property
D. Creditworthiness of the buyer

9. The statement "land cannot be relocated" best illustrates which of the following characteristics of land?

A. Permanence of investment
B. Indestructibility
C. Heterogeneity
D. Immobility

10. All of the following affect supply and demand in the real estate market EXCEPT

A. population migration.
B. tax laws governing real estate transactions.
C. number of real estate agents in the marketplace.
D. environmental conditions.

11. Environmental control, building codes, city planning, and zoning regulations fall under the authority of

A. the allodial system.
B. the feudal system.
C. private land restrictions.
D. government and public land use Controls.

12. All of the following statements regarding the real estate profession are true EXCEPT

A. real estate licensees may specialize in one or more fields.
B. real estate licensees must have a clear picture of the respective roles they play in each transaction.
C. real estate licensees are limited to selling properties.
D. real estate licensees are advisers working diligently to assist all participants in the real estate marketplace.

13. The best example of direct public ownership is:

A. a privately owned auditorium.
B. a subdivision of privately owned homes.
C. utility companies and services.
D. streets, highways, parks.

14. Success in the real estate business is founded upon all of the following EXCEPT

A. ethical conduct.
B. amount of the commission.
C. service to others.
D. knowledge of the market.

15. All of the following are economic characteristics of real estate EXCEPT

A. heterogeneity.
B. location.
C. permanence of investment.
D. scarcity.

16. The real estate market may be described as all of the following EXCEPT

A. local in nature.
B. immobile.
C. cyclical in nature.
D. quick to react.

17. In the feudal system of ownership, land was owned by the ruling powers. Since the 1700's in this country, land may be owned by private individuals. This system of private ownership of land is known as:

A. alluvion.
B. annexation.
C. allodial.
D. anticipation.

18. An investor must consider all of the following before investing in a property EXCEPT

A. highest and best use of improvements.
B. physical and economic characteristics of the property.
C. public or private restrictions on the property.
D. personal objectives.

19. The completion of a real estate transaction occurs at

A. financing.
B. listing.
C. appraisal.
D. settlement.

20. Because financing is so important in most real estate transactions, real estate salespersons should

A. call FHA and VA government offices for an update on local rates.
B. have a day-to-day working knowledge of loan programs.
C. obtain a mortgage broker's license as soon as possible.
D. never recommend seller financing as an alternative to a bank loan.

21. Which of the following terms does NOT define land and everything that is permanently attached to the land?

A. Real property
B. Real estate
C. Realty
D. Personal property

22. "The outlay of money expecting income, or the acquisition of property expecting income or profit" defines

A. mortgage.
B. escrow.
C. equity.
D. investment.

23. An increase in the economic supply of land is created by

A. an increase in the utilization of the land.
B. heterogeneity of land.
C. a decrease in the utilization of the land.
D. location.

24. Which of the following is usually NOT an objective of a real estate investment?

A. Tax shelter
B. Liquidity
C. Hedge against inflation
D. Current or future income

25. All property that is readily movable is known as

A. real estate.
B. realty.
C. real property.
D. personal property.

Property Ownership and Interests

1. Barbie owns four pieces of property in severalty. She marries Ken, and two years later, decides to sell these pieces of her property. According to Michigan law, under these circumstances

A. Ken must sign as a grantor on all properties sold by Barbie.
B. Ken has a life state in remainder in the fourth property.
C. Ken automatically has an entirety interest in the remaining property.
D. Ken has no interest in any of the properties owned by Barbie.

2. Sally conveys 20 acres to Sam for Sam's life. This type of ownership is called a/an

A. estate in severalty.
B. defeasible estate.
C. life estate.
D. estate for years.

3. The difference between a life estate and an estate for years is

A. a life estate creates an estate in reversion whereas the estate for years does not.
B. a life estate is a freehold estate whereas an estate for years is a leasehold estate.
C. a life estate does not convey title whereas an estate for years does convey title.
D. a life estate is not a determinable fee whereas an estate for years is a determinable fee.

4. Which of the following is true about cooperatives but not true about condominiums?

A. Ownership of the interior and the exterior is in the form of tenancy in common
B. The common areas are owned by a corporation in fee
C. The association has right of first refusal to purchase units that are available for sale
D. The master deed must be agreed upon by all occupants

5. An example of an emblement is:

A. jewelry.
B. cash.
C. paddle fans.
D. corn or wheat.

6. Creating a condominium does NOT require recording

A. articles of association.
B. by-laws.
C. a declaration.
D. a mortgage.

7. John Smith buys five pieces of property as a single man, and two years later, marries Sally Jones. He does not put his wife's name on the deeds to the properties. Under these circumstances

A. Sally has a dower interest in all property owned by John.
B. Sally has no interest in the properties purchased by John prior to marriage.
C. Sally has no interest in the properties if she is unaware that they were purchased.
D. Sally will have an interest only at the time of John's death.

44

8. The right of survivorship in real estate can be described as the right of

A. co-owners to automatically receive the interest of the deceased co-owner upon his or her death.
B. a bank to automatically receive ownership upon the death of the mortgagor.
C. two or more people to hold title to a property at the same time.
D. heirs to receive the co-owner's share of real estate as provided in his or her last will and testament.

9. An estate that automatically renews itself for another period at the end of each period unless one party gives notice to the other is termed an

A. estate for years.
B. estate from year to year.
C. estate at will.
D. estate at sufferance.

10. Property owned in a husband's name alone may be sold during his marriage provided

A. his wife signs the deed along with her husband.
B. he receives valuable consideration for the property.
C. it is less than a four-family dwelling.
D. he purchased the property before he got married.

11. The real estate term for improvements both on and to the land is

A. fixtures.
B. emblements.
C. chattel.
D. attachments.

12. The most complete form of estate in real property is which of the following

A. fee simple absolute.
B. qualified fee.
C. leasehold for years.
D. life estate in reversion.

13. When the landlord dies, the estate for years

A. is terminated.
B. is considered void.
C. is binding on the heirs.
D. reverts to a tenancy from month to month.

14. Property that is readily movable and is not attached to the land is called

A. personality.
B. realty.
C. chattel.
D. title.

15. Under the Michigan Dormant Mineral Rights Act, ownership of mineral rights not owned by the property owner must be re-recorded

A. upon the death of the property owners.
B. when they are transferred.
C. once in a lifetime.
D. every 20 years.

16. Gerald conveys a condominium to Felicia for life. Upon Felicia's death, the property goes to Jennifer. Jennifer has an estate in

A. remainder.
B. recession.
C. recision.
D. reversion.

17. Bob and Judy, a brother and sister, own property jointly. They have equal percentages of ownership in the property and they received their title at the same time from the same source. They have the right to undivided possession of the property. If Bob dies, his share will automatically go to Judy and vice versa. The type of concurrent ownership Bob and Judy have is

A. joint tenancy.
B. estate by entireties.
C. estate for years.
D. tenancy in common.

18. By definition, an estate for years

A. requires a written document.
B. must be for at least two years.
C. is for a fixed term whether a week, a month, a year, or longer.
D. must last for one or more years.

19. Growing things that require planting and are usually harvested seasonally are called emblements, whereas growing things that do not require planting but continue to grow naturally (such as perennials) are considered

A. chattel.
B. personal property.
C. real estate.
D. fruits of industry.

20. The most comprehensive form of ownership is known as

A. nonfreehold.
B. joint tenancy.
C. life estate.
D. fee simple absolute.

21. Chattel can be transferred by a document called a/an

A. declaration.
B. bill of sale.
C. mortgage.
D. emblement.

22. Which of the following does NOT refer to a form of concurrent ownership?

A. Estate by entireties
B. Joint tenancy
C. Tenancy in common
D. Tenancy at sufferance

23. Periodic estates and estates for years are examples of which of the following?

A. Freehold
B. Life
C. Dower
D. Leasehold

24. Condominium units that are composed of only vacant land with surface improvements or with airspace within which a building is to be constructed are called

A. subdivision developments.
B. cooperatives.
C. condominium in remainder.
D. site condominiums.

25. The term tenancy in common refers to

A. relationship of renters in an apartment complex.
B. ownership.
C. emblements.
D. survivorship.

26. The most frequently used freehold estate when land is donated to a church, school or community for a specified purpose is

A. dower.
B. qualified fee.
C. life estate.
D. fee simple absolute.

27. Before a timeshare can be offered for sale, its ownership must first be structured as which of the following?

A. Sale of stock
B. Sole proprietorship
C. Condominium
D. Cooperative

28. According to the Michigan Condominium Act, in a new construction condominium sale all documents must be delivered to the purchaser

A. by certified mail only and within 15 days.
B. or to the purchaser's family.
C. in person only.
D. prior to the purchaser being bound to a purchase agreement.

29. The only property interest shareholders in a cooperative have is

A. the right of first refusal.
B. a leasehold estate.
C. the title to the property.
D. fee simple absolute.

30. A security agreement allows a lender to retain a security interest in a business owner's personal property until the lender is paid in full in accordance with

A. business partnership agreement.
B. Uniform Commercial Code.

C. Trade Fixture Agreement Act.
D. Chattels on Loan Law.

31. A leasehold estate that has a definite termination date is known as a/an

A. estate at will.
B. estate for years.
C. tenancy in common.
D. estate at sufferance.

32. Virginia and Bill own property jointly. Virginia owns 80 percent while Bill owns 20 percent. Upon death, Virginia's interest in the property will go to her favorite charity whereas Bill's ownership interest will go to his wife. The type of concurrent ownership Virginia and Bill have is

A. estate for years.
B. estate by the entireties.
C. tenancy in common.
D. joint tenancy.

33. A business operator may remove certain items attached to the real property at the time of sale. These items are referred to as

A. chattel.
B. trade fixtures.
C. emblements.
D. real estate.

34. A person's right or interest in real property is known as his or her

A. chattel.
B. estate.
C. dower rights.
D. personalty.

35. A fee simple estate with a condition or limitation attached is termed a/an

A. estate in severalty.
B. defeasible estate.
C. life estate.
D. estate for years.

36. Sam was in lawful possession of Larry's property but now refuses to leave after his right to possession has been terminated. Sam is known as which of the following type of tenant?

A. At years
B. At severalty
C. At sufferance
D. At will

37. Under most circumstances all of the following MUST be given to a purchase of a new construction condominium prior to the purchaser being bound to a purchase agreement EXCEPT

A. a copy of the purchase and escrow agreements.
B. Condominium Buyer's Handbook.
C. proprietary lease.
D. disclosure statement.

38. Joanne and Don owned property as tenants by the entirety (husband and wife). Upon their divorce they agreed to continue their ownership of the property. Their tenants by the entirety ownership is automatically changed to

A. joint tenancy.
B. estate for years.
C. tenancy in common.
D. estate by entireties.

39. Which of the following is the opposite of co-ownership?

A. Ownership in severalty
B. Tenancy in common
C. Joint tenancy
D. Estate by entireties

40. The declaration or master deed to a condominium may contain everything EXCEPT

A. the height, width, and length of each unit.
B. the legal description of the condominium facility.
C. owner's names.
D. a right of first refusal clause.

41. Which of the following is NOT true about condominiums?

A. Ownership of space in a multi-unit structure is fee simple ownership
B. Owners are subject to certain controls by the condominium association
C. No deduction of taxes or mortgage interest is allowed to condominium owners
D. Owners or developers record a signed and notarized declaration of condominium

42. The law that governs the financing of personal property is called the

A. Statute of Limitations.
B. Uniform Commercial Code.
C. bill of sale.
D. Statute of Frauds.

43. The form of concurrent ownership that requires the unities of time, title, interest, and possession is

A. ownership in severalty.
B. joint tenancy.
C. tenancy in common.
D. ownership in remainder.

44. Which of the following is NOT true about a fee simple estate?

A. It is a type of freehold estate
B. It is the most comprehensive and simplest form of title
C. It includes the right to dispose of the Property
D. It must be conveyed as estate in severalty

45. Fee simple estate and life estate are two examples of which of the following estates

A. periodic.
B. nonfreehold.
C. freehold.
D. leasehold.

Michigan Real Estate License Laws and Rules

1. The Department has the authority to do all of the following EXCEPT

A. discipline licensees who commit license law violations.
B. dictate the length of a prison term for violators.
C. issue licenses to qualified applicants.
D. suspend or revoke licenses.

2. Act 299 requires a broker to deposit all third-party money coming into his possession

A. at any time prior to the closing.
B. no later than two days from receipt of the buyer's offer.
C. within two banking days from the broker's knowledge of an accepted offer.
D. within five days from the seller's acceptance of an offer.

3. Michigan License Law requires a broker to supervise her agents. Which of the following indicates a lack of supervision?

A. She allowed her agents to sell more than five houses a year
B. She allowed her agents to sign escrow checks without her signature, too
C. She provided her agents with predetermined policies
D. She had all her agents sign independent contractor contracts

4. Earl Eager has never held a real estate license but has been buying and selling houses as investments for several years. In the past year he personally negotiated 15 transactions. He decides to open an investment company to show other people how to buy and sell real estate. He realizes he must have a broker's license. He knows that the department will grant 6 months' credit toward a broker's license for every 5 personally negotiated transactions. He sends documentation to the department proving the 15 transactions were personally negotiated by him. Which of the following best applies to this situation?

A. Earl will receive one year's credit toward his broker's license because the maximum credit for an investor is one year
B. Earl will receive one and one-half

49

years' credit toward his broker's license

C. Earl will need to prove only an additional one and one-half years experience, 90 clock hours of classroom study, and successfully complete the broker's exam to obtain his broker's license

D. Earl will receive no credit toward his broker's license and may be found in violation of license law for practicing real estate without a license

5. All of the following are license law violations EXCEPT

A. making a false promise to induce someone to sign a contract.
B. making a substantial and willful misrepresentation.
C. paying an unlicensed person for services in the real estate transaction.
D. selling your own listing.

6. The following ad appeared in a local newspaper: "Beautiful Cape Cod 3 bdrms, full bsmnt. Call Gary Beanie." Which of the following is true?

A. Beanie could be a salesperson
B. Beanie could advertise this way with the permission of the department
C. Beanie cannot be a licensee
D. Beanie could be a broker

7. A licensee will be subject to the penalties set forth in Article 6 by engaging in any of the following EXCEPT

A. failing to disclose to a purchaser or lessee of real property that a former occupant has or is suspected of having a disability.

B. failing to provide a written agency disclosure to a prospective buyer or seller in a real estate transaction.
C. acting for more than one party in a transaction without the knowledge of the parties.
D. changing a business location without notification to the department.

8. Sally B. Leevan has three transactions pending at the time she informs her broker that she is leaving. She requests that her broker pay her at the closing of those transactions, even though she will not be licensed at that office when the closings take place. Which of the following applies?

A. The broker must turn the transactions over to another agent in the office and require Sally and the other agent to split the commissions
B. The broker is allowed to pay Sally after she leaves for commissions earned while she was licensed there
C. The broker must keep the commission in the escrow until Sally comes back
D. The broker cannot pay Sally because license law dictates that a broker can pay only licensees of the broker

9. An individual who operates under a duly executed power of attorney is known as a/an

A. attorney-in-fact.
B. real estate broker.
C. attorney-at-law.
D. general fiduciary of the seller.

10. A Michigan broker who wishes to promote in Michigan the sale of land located in another state MUST do all of the following EXCEPT

A. comply with all rules, restrictions, and conditions set by the department.
B. pay all expenses incurred by the department in investigating the promotion.
C. submit full particulars regarding the property to the department.
D. be a licensed broker in both states.

11. Michigan license law allows a licensee to do any of the following EXCEPT

A. appraise real estate.
B. put buyers under contract and be entitled to a fee when a buyer purchases a house.
C. manage property.
D. sell the business of a property owner who wants to retain the real estate.

12. Agent Lucky Lasar writes an offer on one of his own listings. Within the following seven days the offer is countered between the buyer and seller four different times. The seller finally accepts a counter from the buyer. Agent Lasar then deposits the earnest money. Which of the following is true?

A. The agent's broker would have no liability because he was not aware of the transaction.
B. As long as the deposit was in the form of a certified check the agent acted in good faith
C. The agent has acted in compliance with the license law because he has deposited the earnest money within two banking days of the broker's knowledge of an accepted offer

D. The agent is in violation of the license law because the earnest money should have been deposited within five days of receipt regardless of the date of the seller's acceptance

13. A salesperson has been asked by a licensed builder to sell houses in the builder's new subdivision. The builder indicates the willingness to pay a commission plus a bonus for all the extras the salesperson sells with the houses. Based on these facts, which of the following is true?

A. All monies owed to the salesperson must be paid by the salesperson's employing broker
B. Because the builder is licensed, the commissions and bonuses may be paid directly to the salesperson
C. The builder must receive written permission from the salesperson's broker to pay the salesperson directly
D. The salesperson must inform the builder that the commission checks must be issued to the salesperson's broker; however, the salesperson may receive the bonus money directly

14. A salesperson who wishes to transfer her license to another broker MUST do all of the following EXCEPT

A. have the new broker sign and date her pocket card and write her ID number on it.
B. submit a transfer form to the department with the proper fees.
C. personally sign and date the back of her pocket card.
D. send her pocket card to the department for transfer.

15. A person appointed to perform for another under duly executed power of attorney is known as a/an

A. agent.
B. attorney-at-law.
C. representative.
D. attorney-in-fact.

16. Persons exempt from real estate license requirements include all of the following EXCEPT

A. receivers.
B. attorneys-in-fact.
C. trustees in bankruptcy.
D. part-time salespersons.

17. A broker has 80 licensees in his office. He decides to put all their licenses in a book and keep the book in his office so he can easily access their license numbers. According to license law the broker

A. can handle the licenses in this fashion provided he makes them available to anyone who wants to see them.
B. should have each agent hold his own license.
C. must conspicuously display all licenses.
D. has custody of all licenses and must have them in his personal possession.

18. A seller accepts an offer on a Monday. On Wednesday the seller's agent receives an offer that is $5,000 higher than the offer that has already been accepted. The listing contract with the seller contains NO provision that the broker shall not continue to market the property once an offer has been accepted. Under these circumstances, which of the following is true?

A. The agent should advise the first buyer to raise his offer by $6,000
B. The agent must present the second offer to the seller
C. The agent should present the second offer to the seller and recommend they cancel the first offer
D. The agent has no obligation to the seller to present the second offer

19. After completing the 40-hour pre-licensing course, a salesperson successfully completes the licensing exam. She does not have a broker for whom she is going to work. In this situation the department will

A. require verification that she completed the 40 hours within 30 days prior to taking the exam.
B. require that she take the test again when she finds an employing broker.
C. issue a license at any time in the future when she finds an employing broker.
D. hold the results of the exam for one year and issue a license when she finds an employing broker within that year.

20. Melissa Talast, a salesperson, sells over $20 million in real estate every year. She is concerned about her exposure to liability and how it could affect her income. After consulting with her attorney and accountant, she decides to incorporate to reduce her risk of liability. She informs her broker that from now on, she wants her commission checks made out of her corporation. Which of the following is true?

A. The broker may write the checks to Melissa's corporation after sending written documentation to the department explaining the situation
B. The broker must issue check payable

to the name under which the salesperson's license is issued, and the salesperson may conduct business only in the name under which her license is issued

C. The described situation is allowable under Michigan license law
D. The salesperson must first obtain an associate broker's license, and then she will be permitted to incorporate

21. Richard Diamond obtains a listing in which the seller requests that the broker not put the listing on the multi-list and not offer cooperation and compensation to other agents. A salesperson from another office notices the "for sale" sign, and when he calls to make appointment, is informed by Mr. Diamond that there is no cooperative relationship offered. The salesperson files a complaint with the department. Which of the following is true?

A. Richard should ask the other agent to refer the buyer and then Richard must pay a fee to the agent
B. Richard does not have a valid listing and therefore must give his commission back to the seller
C. Richard has not violated license law because he did not promise that he would cooperate with other brokers
D. Richard is in violation of license law because he is a participant in a multiple listing service and must therefore cooperate with all brokers

22. An authorized representative of the department calls a broker and asks her to meet him at a restaurant near her office and to bring all transaction records from the last six months. The representative explains that it would be better to meet there to avoid the embarrassment of the broker's agents finding out she is being

investigated. Under these circumstances, the broker

A. must comply with the request of the representative.
B. should ask her office manager to accompany her as a witness.
C. does not have to comply with the representative's request.
D. has five days to show cause as to why she will not comply.

23. In order to obtain a real estate license, an applicant must pass a written exam in all cases EXCEPT if the applicant

A. has been practicing investment real estate.
B. is an attorney-at-law who wants to obtain a broker's license.
C. inherited the real estate office from his parents.
D. has a provable, documentable disability that prevents writing.

24. A listing salesperson may receive compensation for services rendered in marketing real estate from

A. his employing broker.
B. the buyer.
C. the cooperating broker.
D. the seller.

25. Broker M.T. Pockets has 25 licensees in his office. Six of them are non-principal associate brokers, and the other 19 are salespeople. Broker Pockets occasionally writes checks to himself out of his escrow account. The department's audit of his books shows that in the past year he has taken over $300,000 that didn't belong to him. After a hearing, the department decides to revoke Pocket's broker's license. Under these

circumstances which of the following is true?

A. All licenses in Broker Pocket's office are automatically suspended
B. All associate brokers' licenses in the office are revoked along with Broker Pocket's license
C. All licensees in the office are responsible for replacing the escrow monies
D. The salesperson must choose a new broker to run the office

26. Clara Darvin, a licensed salesperson, buys a home. Which of the following is true regarding such a transaction?

A. Darvin has the right to receive a commission for both the listing and the sale
B. Darvin's broker may pay her without the seller's consent
C. Darvin is allowed to accept a commission if it is her own listing
D. Darvin may not accept a commission on such a transaction without the written consent of the seller

27. To be qualified as a real estate licensee, applicants must have all of the following EXCEPT

A. a working knowledge of the state license law.
B. knowledge of real estate.
C. membership in an MLS and knowledge of its regulations.
D. reputation for honesty and fair dealing.

28. Is an associate broker a broker?

A. An associate broker is a broker because the requirements for a broker's license have been met
B. There is no way an associate broker can be a broker
C. An associate broker is a broker if there are no more than five associate brokers in the office
D. An associate broker is a broker if the individual proves an additional three years of experience in the field of real estate

29. A person licensed as a practitioner and living in another state who wants to conduct real estate business in Michigan must do all of the following EXCEPT

A. successfully complete the Michigan state exam.
B. sign an irrevocable consent to service of process.
C. complete the required clock hours of education.
D. become a resident of the state of Michigan.

30. Salesperson Chris Fraser goes to a closing with the necessary closing statements signed by his broker. During the closing, it becomes necessary to change the figures on the statement. Fraser may do so provided

A. the buyer and seller both sign a statement allowing him to do so.
B. under no circumstances can he or his broker change the statement.
C. the total dollar amount does not exceed $3,000.
D. he does so under the direct supervision of his broker.

31. "Any person, partnership, association or corporation who transacts real estate for a fee for others" defines a/an

A. salesperson.
B. broker.
C. owner.
D. commissioner.

32. Quinton Alexander, a gifted child, graduated from law school at the age of 15. He worked full-time in a real estate law firm for three years. After his eighteenth birthday, he decided to get his real estate broker's license. Which of the following is true?

A. He must first be a full-time salesperson for 3 years, obtain 90 clock hours of classroom study, and successfully complete the broker's exam
B. There is no way he can obtain a broker's license at the age of 18
C. He will receive 60 clock hours toward his broker's license for obtaining a law degree, and the department will recognize his 3 years of full-time experience. Therefore, to receive a broker's license, all he needs is another 30 clock hours of classroom study and successful completion of the broker's exam
D. He can only be an associate broker under another supervisory broker until he is 21

33. A salesperson can do all of the following EXCEPT

A. show a property to his customers.
B. own and operate a real estate business as a sole proprietor.
C. farm areas to generate listings.

D. advertise his listing using the name of the broker.

34. Betty and Bob are getting a divorce. Betty's attorney has advised her to ask a real estate broker the value of the couple's property. The broker advises Betty that he charges a $250 fee for this service. According to Michigan license law

A. only an attorney for one of the divorcees can do the market analysis.
B. a market analysis is an appraisal; therefore, the broker must be a licensed appraiser.
C. the broker may charge a fee for a market analysis if it does not involve a federally related transaction.
D. the broker cannot charge any fee other than his commission for the sale of the property.

35. Salesperson Adams assures a prospective purchaser that the owners have had no problems with water in the basement of their home when in fact the salesperson has been informed by the sellers that they installed a sump pump last year because of frequent basement flooding. Upon learning from the salesperson that no problem exists, the buyers decide to start negotiations to purchase this property. What effect could the salesperson's statement have upon her license?

A. She may have to apologize to the buyers immediately
B. She may lose her license because of misrepresentation
C. No effect because the sump pump has been installed
D. No effect until the basement floods again

36. Agents must carry their pocket card

A. only when conducting business authorized by the broker.
B. at all times.
C. at all times when acting in the capacity indicated on the pocket card.
D. only when listing or selling houses.

37. Peter, Paul and Mary decide they want to open a real estate company. They want to make it a limited partnership called Pine Tree Real Estate, Ltd., with Peter as the general partner. In order to receive a broker's license for their company

A. Paul and Mary cannot be active in the real estate business.
B. Pine Tree Real Estate must be a corporation, and Peter, Paul, and Mary must be licensed associate brokers as the officers of the corporation.
C. Peter must be an associate broker.
D. Peter, Paul, and Mary must all be licensed associate brokers.

38. Michigan license law requires

A. a licensee to verbally tell a buyer that the licensee is the owner when selling her own property.
B. no disclosure when a licensee's spouse is purchasing real estate.
C. no disclosure if a licensee is indirectly involved in a purchase.
D. written disclosure to be made to a seller or buyer that the party buying or selling, respectively, is a licensee, prior to any transaction taking place.

39. State license law requires the licensee to do all of the following EXCEPT

A. follow state statutes regarding real estate licensing.
B. join the local association of REALTORS®.
C. possess knowledge and skill necessary to enter the real estate business.
D. possess a reputation for honesty and fair dealing.

40. A false statement regarding an important matter in a real estate transaction to induce someone to enter into a contract is called

A. "buyer beware."
B. reciprocity.
C. the unauthorized practice of law.
D. misrepresentation.

41. At the listing presentation, an agent advises the sellers that the agent will fill in the area of the listing contract that provides the square footage and remarks on the property when the agent gets back to his office. Additionally, he tells the sellers that he is leaving the expiration date blank so that they only need to call him to take the property off the market. Which of following is true?

A. The listing must contain a definite expiration date and be completely. filled out prior to the seller's signing
B. The agent is exercising good business judgment by allowing himself time to do ample research on the property. and giving the sellers a quick way to get their property off the market.

C. The agent can leave the square footage and remarks open but must fill in the expiration date.
D. The agent has a net listing on the property.

42. The state's authority to require real estate licensure falls under

A. police power.
B. housing codes.
C. taxation boards.
D. zoning boards.

43. A buyer is negotiating directly with a developer to purchase a home in a new subdivision. The buyer has hired a real estate broker as his consultant to help him understand the documents and clauses of a contract given by the developer. After reviewing the documents the broker states that everything appears to be complete, but she suggests that a purchase money mortgage would be better than the land contract to which the developer and purchaser have agreed and also suggests that she, the broker, draw up the contract. The broker has violated the license law by

A. giving unauthorized legal counsel.
B. representing a buyer.
C. being hired as a consultant.
D. not representing the seller.

44. Michigan license law may require all of the following EXCEPT

A. verification of reputation.
B. membership in NAR.
C. written examination.
D. course of study.

Agency

1. MOST relationships in real estate brokerage are

A. general agencies.
B. universal agencies.
C. special agencies.
D. dual agencies.

2. Which of the following statements is true regarding an agency relationship?

A. The brokerage may never participate in dual agency.
B. An agency relationship must be in writing for the agent to have any liability to the principal.
C. The agent's principal is also referred to as the customer.
D. An agency relationship can be established by the conduct of the parties.

3. Which of the following persons would best be described as a subagent?

A. Buyer
B. Selling broker
C. Listing broker
D. Seller

4. The person that an agent represents in a transaction is determined by

A. who is paying the agent compensation.
B. the contract and/or the conduct of the Agent.
C. state law.
D. the Board of REALTORS® MLS Agreement.

5. An agent sells a house and is now working with the sellers to find another house. The agent is not acting as a buyer's broker. During the time their house was listed, the agent learned that the buyers had just received a substantial inheritance. They are now going to make an offer that is $40,000 under the asking price of a piece of property. Under these circumstances, the agent MUST

A. present the offer as submitted and keep all confidential information he learned during another agency relationship confidential indefinitely.
B. advise the buyers that he will not present an offer that far below list price.
C. disclose this information to the sellers because they are his clients.
D. tell the sellers to counter the offer because the buyers are loaded.

6. Michigan law mandates that agency disclosure by a real estate licensee to a potential buyer or seller must be completed

A. before any contractual agreement is entered into between the parties.
B. after the agent shows the buyer no more than three properties.
C. before the disclosure of confidential information.
D. at the discretion of the broker.

7. An office that has one broker and seventeen salespeople would not be a/an

A. brokerage firm.
B. franchise.
C. multiple listing service.
D. independent brokerage.

8. When the conduct of the salesperson indicates an agency relationship but there is no formal contract this might be called any of these EXCEPT

A. unintentional agency.
B. accidental agency.
C. implied agency.
D. express agency.

9. A sales agent in one office of Martinelli Realty has a listing. A salesperson in another branch of Martinelli Realty has a buyer for his listing and is working as a buyer's broker. Which of these statements is correct about their agency relationships?

A. Two single agency relationships are in place because there are two different sales agents involved.
B. Martinelli Realty can receive compensation only from either the buyer or the seller, but not both
C. The buyer has customer status
D. There is dual agency because Martinelli Realty is the agent of both Parties

10. Seller Jamison has instructed broker Jordan not to tell any buyers that a room addition was done by Jamison himself. Jamison is excellent with carpentry, drywall and painting, but had no prior experience with electrical work. Broker Jordan tests all the plugs and switches and they all work fine. Six months later, the home purchaser uses all the plugs at once suffers a small fire in the wall with $4,000 damage. Jordan is guilty of

A. caveat emptor.
B. no wrongdoing.
C. freehold.
D. misrepresentation.

11. A system that pools the listings of all member firms is known as

A. general agreement.
B. universal agency.
C. sub-agency.
D. multiple listing service.

12. The commission to be paid to a broker is

A. a set rate determined by a local board of brokers.
B. set by state law.
C. paid by the seller.
D. negotiated between the broker and the client. The amount of the commission is stipulated in the agency contract.

13. Agent Anderson receives a $2,000 earnest money deposit from a buyer on Monday. The seller is on vacation for three weeks. Under these circumstances, agent Anderson should

A. give the deposit back to the buyer until the seller returns to town.
B. deposit the check in his own checking account until the offer is presented.
C. instruct the buyer to postdate the check.
D. turn the check over to his broker.

14. To make agency relationships clear to the largest number of people in the largest number of transactions, agency disclosure forms are required

A. only if an agent represents the buyer and not the seller as is customary.
B. only during a cooperative transaction between two brokerages.
C. only if there is a dual agency.
D. in all transactions regardless of whom the agent represents.

15. When listing the seller's home a broker notices and asks about several water spots on the living room ceiling. The seller says that the leak has been fixed and subsequently paints the ceiling. Assuming the leak has been fixed, the broker does not mention this to the buyer. After closing, the roof leaks. The broker is guilty of

A. a positive misrepresentation.
B. an innocent misrepresentation.
C. breach of fiduciary duty.
D. habendum.

16. An agent working with a buyer to locate a property

A. may accept compensation from either the buyer or the seller or both (with disclosure and their consent).
B. must not accept compensation from the buyer.
C. may have a buyer's brokerage contract but then cannot be paid by the seller.
D. must not accept compensation from the seller.

17. If an agent is found guilty for violating the Michigan Anti-Trust Act, he is subject to all of the following EXCEPT

A. mandatory probation by the department.
B. felony conviction.
C. treble damages to the injured party.
D. a fine not to exceed $100,000 per violation.

18. Under buyer agency the

A. buyer always pays for his broker's commission.
B. buyer's broker may not be compensated by the seller.

C. buyer's broker's commission may be paid by either party as determined through the negotiations.

D. seller must pay the buyer's broker's commission.

19. Sandy and Bruce are sales associates in the same brokerage. The broker's agency policy states that the firm will represent buyers and sellers under contract. On Monday Sandy brings in a listing. On Friday Bruce puts a buyer under contract. That weekend Bruce shows Sandy's listing to his buyer, who ultimately writes an offer. In this case

A. broker must tell the buyer to go to another company to complete the transaction.
B. broker is in a dual agency situation and all parties must be informed and give their consent in writing.
C. Sandy and Bruce can not split the Commission.
D. Sandy is representing only the seller and Bruce is representing only the buyer.

20. After walking through an open house one Sunday, the prospective buyer informs the listing agent, who is present, that this is the house she wants to buy. Which of the following represents the next step that the agent should take?

A. Explain agency and provide the buyer with a signed agency disclosure statement
B. Immediately provide the buyer with the seller's disclosure statement
C. Call a mortgage representative to have the buyer qualified
D. Discuss the price and terms with the buyer

21. A buyer's agent MUST disclose her agency relationship to a cooperating broker

A. at the presentation of an offer.
B. prior to a purchase agreement being signed.
C. before the closing.
D. at first contact with the cooperating broker.

22. When both parties to a transaction (buyer and seller) are expressly represented by one brokerage even though the representation is by two different salespeople at the brokerage, there exists a(n)

A. dual agency.
B. ostensible agency.
C. illegal agency.
D. multiple agency.

23. A buyer employing a broker ONLY to assist in finding a certain type of property to purchase has authorized a/an

A. special agency.
B. attorney-in-fact.
C. power of attorney.
D. general agency.

24. A buyer and seller enter into a purchase agreement. Three days after the signing of the contract, the seller hands the buyer, in person, a copy of the mandatory Seller Disclosure Form. Under these circumstances the

A. buyer has no recourse.
B. buyer has 72 hours from delivery of the statement to terminate the contract in writing.
C. contract is automatically invalidated.
D. seller is not in violation of the Michigan's Seller Disclosure Act.

25. An agency relationship may be terminated by any of the following EXCEPT

A. death of either the principal or the agent.
B. completion of the contract.
C. estoppel.
D. expiration of the contract.

26. The Michigan's Seller's Disclosure Act requires real estate practitioners to

A. make the Seller's Disclosure Form available.
B. assist the seller, if they are a client, in filling out the form.
C. advise a buyer-client to rely on whatever the seller put on the form as being fact.
D. immediately cancel the listing if the seller fills the form out wrong.

27. Under agency law, which of the following statements is NOT true?

A. In a special agency relationship, the broker can bind the principal to a contract
B. The principal may be the seller
C. A universal agency can create an attorney-in-fact
D. Under general agency, the agent may bind the principal to a contract

28. An agent representing the seller has which of the following duties to both the buyer and the seller?

A. Loyalty
B. Care
C. Disclosure
D. Skill

29. Seller Armstrong, in an effort to get rid of a pestering broker who claims to have a buyer for Armstrong's land, tells the broker that all of his real estate dealings are handled by Jenkins Realty. Even though there is no formal agency contract with Jenkins Realty, Armstrong may have created an agency by

A. estoppel.
B. misrepresentation.
C. extension.
D. authority.

30. Commissions charged by brokers may be established by any of the following EXCEPT

A. percentage of the asking price in the listing agreement.
B. policy agreement between brokers who are members of the Board of REALTORS®.
C. flat fee agreement.
D. buyer brokerage agreement.

31. An agent has failed to inform the buyer of the fact that the home is not on the city sewer system, but instead has a septic system. The agent knew this and simply forgot to tell the buyer. Which of these statements is true?

A. The buyer would have no recourse under the principle of "caveat emptor," or "buyer beware"
B. The agent has misrepresented to the buyer through this act of omission
C. The agent has done nothing wrong because the agent did not actually say anything one way or the other and no one asked
D. The agent is guilty of fraud

32. Which of these duties does a principal have to an agent representing him?

A. Cooperation
B. Accounting
C. Loyalty
D. Exclusively

33. When a broker commingles funds of his clients and customers within his operating account, he has violated his duty of

A. accounting.
B. loyalty.
C. disclosure.
D. care.

34. An agent's fiduciary duty is to the

A. seller.
B. client.
C. customer.
D. buyer.

35. A properly licensed salesperson

A. may take deposits and place them into his trust account.
B. who is switching to a different brokerage may take any of his listings to the new brokerage.
C. may place real estate advertisements at his own discretion.
D. must conduct all aspects of his business under the direction of the broker.

36. Which type of commission structure is illegal in Michigan?

A. Net listing
B. Flat fee listing
C. Percentage listing
D. Multiple listing

37. Broker Jenson and Seller Stein have signed a listing agreement. Jenson's agency relationship with Stein is best described as

A. special agency.
B. implied agency.
C. general agency.
D. universal agency.

38. Historically the most common type of agency agreement is a/an

A. agency by estoppel.
B. listing agreement between broker and seller.
C. implied general agency for broker to represent seller.
D. buyer brokerage agreement.

39. Regarding real estate commissions and compensation, which of the following is INCORRECT?

A. Antitrust laws prohibit competing brokers from collectively collaborating on the amount of commission percentage to charge
B. A broker may elect to charge different commission percentages for different types of properties based on price, location, or class
C. A brokerage firm, not the salesperson, owns the listings
D. A broker is not entitled to a commission even if the seller refuses to complete the transaction with a ready, willing, and able buyer

40. An agency relationship is created

A. by the fact that the agent has a real estate license.
B. with a written contract between the agent and the principal.
C. through either a contract with a principal or the conduct and actions of the parties.
D. by the conduct of the agent

41. The process of bringing buyers and sellers together and assisting in the negotiations during the real estate transaction is called

A. brokerage.
B. marketing.
C. listing.
D. selling.

42. A multiple listing service

A. violates antitrust law because of broker collusion.
B. may result in a more thorough marketing of listed properties throughout local markets.
C. requires buyer's brokerage by the cooperating agents.
D. requires sub-agency by the cooperating brokers.

43. Fiduciary duties of an agent do NOT include

A. estoppel.
B. loyalty.
C. skill.
D. disclosure.

44. Seller Johnson tells broker Armstrong not to disclose that there are electrical

problems with the two smaller bedroom circuits. The most relevant duty of broker Armstrong is

A. fair dealing and disclosure of this fact to the buyer.
B. loyalty to the seller.
C. care to represent the seller.
D. obedience to the seller.

Fair Housing

1. Which of the following is NOT a protected class under the 1968 Fair Housing Act?

A. Religion
B. Color
C. Familial status
D. Race

2. The Civil Rights Act of 1968 added the prohibition of discrimination in housing based upon

A. familial status.
B. religion.
C. sex.
D. race.

3. In a state where the fair housing law is comparable to the federal Fair Housing Act, complaints based on the federal law must first be

A. referred to the state enforcement agency.
B. published in the local newspaper.
C. mediated before a municipal housing authority.
D. forwarded directly to the federal court.

4. Enforcement of the Fair Housing Act through HUD can include all of the following EXCEPT

A. revocation of real estate license.
B. financial penalties of $10,000 to $50,000 by an administrative law judge.
C. civil suit in federal court.
D. action by the U.S. Attorney General.

5. The Americans with Disabilities Act applies to

A. owners and operators of commercial facilities as long as they employ more than 15 people.
B. veterans of foreign wars only.
C. owners and operators of private accommodations.
D. local and state governments.

6. Landlords can use the phrase "adults only" to

A. advertising older-residential housing if 50 percent of the units have persons age 55 or older.
B. discriminate against a person who is pregnant.
C. discriminate against an adult with children under 18.
D. advertise senior citizen housing if all units are occupied by individuals age 62 or older.

7. If a seller requests that a real estate salesperson not show the seller's property to minorities, the salesperson should

A. follow the seller's instructions.
B. withdraw from the listing relationship.

C. report the seller to HUD.
D. advise the seller to try another broker.

8. Real estate brokerage firms are required by federal law to display the Fair Housing poster

A. in a prominent manner.
B. in all advertising.
C. anywhere in the office.
D. by giving a copy to each client.

9. State civil rights laws

A. can increase the exemptions found under federal law.
B. can add protected classes to those specified by the federal law.
C. can not be enforced through injunctive relief or damages.
D. can not add more protected classes to the federal law.

10. Mr. and Mrs. Humphrey and their two children are transferred to a new town and wish to purchase a house. They view several properties with an agent and decide to make an offer on one of them. The agent indicates that the neighborhood is very quiet and that perhaps the children would not have any playmates. The Humphreys insist that the agent present their offer. The offer is rejected, and the agent tells the buyers that the sellers were very uncomfortable selling the house to a family with children because all of their neighbors are retirees. This is

A. a violation of 1988 amendments to the federal Fair Housing Act.
B. a situation in which the sellers are right to take this position.
C. no violation of any fair housing laws.
D. a violation of the Civil Rights Act of 1866.

11. The Fair Housing Amendments of 1988 include all of the following provisions EXCEPT

A. an increase in fines.
B. addition of protected classes; familial status and disability.
C. allowance for HUD to refer complaints to an ALJ.
D. a requirement that the injured party submit to mediation.

12. Which of the following programs provides funding for civil rights testers?

A. The Americans with Disabilities Act
B. The Fair Housing Initiative Program
C. The National Association for Integration
D. The voluntary Affirmative Marketing Program

13. Which of the following is NOT a protected class under the 1968 Fair Housing Act?

A. Race
B. Color
C. Sex
D. Religion

14. The Fair Housing Amendments of 1988 provide that the landlord who has a tenant with disabilities must

A. give permission to the tenant with disabilities to renovate the premises to accommodate his or her life functions at the tenant's cost.
B. grant permission to the tenant to make necessary modifications at the landlord's expense.
C. provide whatever adjustments are needed to fit the life functions of the tenant.
D. make minor modifications to accommodate the life functions of the person with disabilities.

15. Directing prospective minority purchasers to presently integrated areas to avoid integration of nonintegrated areas is called

A. redlining.
B. blockbusting.
C. steering.
D. violation of the ADA.

16. Which of the following is NOT an example of steering?

A. Showing Hispanic buyers properties only in primarily Hispanic neighborhoods
B. Having one swimming pool for "Adults Only"
C. Showing upper-income buyers luxury properties only
D. Showing African-American prospects properties only in integrated areas

17. Refusing to make loans within certain geographical boundaries by discriminating on the basis of race, color, religion, sex, national origin, disability, or familial status is termed

A. blockbusting.
B. steering.
C. mortgaging.
D. redlining.

18. All of the following were designed to implement the Fair Housing Act EXCEPT

A. Voluntary Affirmative Marketing Program.
B. Fair Housing Initiative Program.
C. Elliot-Larsen Civil Rights Act.
D. Civil Rights Act of 1866.

19. The Fair Housing Act of 1968 was amended in 1988 to include

A. familial status and mental and physical disability.
B. pets.
C. race, color, and national origin.
D. religion and sex.

20. Which of the following is NOT an example of discriminatory advertising in the sale or rental of residential property?

A. "Adults only"
B. "Male college students only"
C. "Non smokers preferred"
D. "No Puerto Ricans"

21. Real estate salespeople should be well-informed on civil rights laws because discrimination

A. is socially offensive.
B. can expose one to legal liability.
C. can jeopardize a transaction.
D. classes are required for license renewal.

22. In the Americans with Disabilities Act, a mental or physical impairment that hampers any life functions is referred to as

A. a special need.
B. discrimination.
C. a disability.
D. steering.

23. Which of the following is NOT exempt from the 1968 Fair Housing Act?

A. Real estate owners of not more than three single-family dwellings at any one time
B. A private club not open to the public if the club owns property for non commercial lodging purposes
C. A religious organization if properties are owned and operated for the benefit of members for non commercial purposes
D. Real estate brokers providing brokerage services

24. When choosing properties to show a prospective buyer, a real estate salesperson can legally take into account any of the following EXCEPT

A. financial obligations.
B. sex.
C. income.
D. occupation.

25. All of the following are illegal EXCEPT

A. refusing to rent to a family with children.
B. advising a prospective buyer of a different national origin than others in a given neighborhood that a house has been sold when it is still available.
C. refusing to accept an offer to purchase because the offeror is a member of a certain religion.
D. refusing to rent to a person with a dog.

26. Which of the following statements is NOT true regarding the Civil Rights Act of 1866?
A. The 1866 law has no exemption provision
B. All citizens have the same rights to inherit, buy, sell, and lease real and personal property
C. This statute is designed to prohibit discrimination because of race
D. Because this law was enacted so long ago, it is now obsolete

27. The ADA is enforceable by all of the following actions EXCEPT

A. a jail sentence for the first offense.
B. a fine of $100,000 for subsequent offenses.
C. a fine of $50,000 for the first offense.
D. Injunctions against operations of a business.

28. If a complaint is filed under the Elliott-Larsen Civil Rights Act, the complaint must be filed within

A. 90 days from the alleged discrimination.
B. any time after the alleged discrimination.
C. 180 days from the alleged discrimination.
D. 365 days from the alleged discrimination.

29. Broker Jones runs the following ad: "Beautiful three bedrooms, brick ranch in prestigious Pine Tree Acres Subdivision. Ideal for young couples. This ad could trigger an investigation for violation of the federal Fair Housing Act of 1968 because the

A. ad is not grammatically correct.
B. ad does not indicate that retirees would enjoy this property.
C. terms "prestigious" and "young couples" could be viewed as indicating a preference for a certain classification.
D. the broker is not advertising the price.

30. Which of the following is an example of blockbusting?

A. Warning a seller to place her home up for sale because minorities are moving into the area
B. Having a welcome party for new neighbors
C. Advertising "Integrated Neighborhood"
D. Showing white buyers properties only in areas populated by white people

31. At the end of a lease a person with disabilities who has made changes to the unit to fit his special needs must

A. return the premises to their original condition.
B. leave the premises with the alterations intact.
C. be reimbursed for any expenses incurred by the changes.
D. give sufficient time for the landlord to return the premises to their original condition.

32. Broker Langley canvassed a subdivision to inform her former customers about the plan for construction of a complex of affordable housing for Russian immigrants adjacent to their subdivision. As a result, many owners expressed concern that this would cause a loss in value of their property. The broker agreed with them and suggested it might be a good time to sell their property. She informed them about a new subdivision she had just listed in another part of town. The broker may be guilty of

A. steering.
B. blockbusting.
C. redlining.
D. farming.

33. Ms. Martinez has inherited a home for which she has placed an ad in the newspaper for tenants. One of the applicants is Asian. She refuses to rent to this woman because she prefers renters of her own national origin with whom she shares a common cultural background.

What part of the law has Ms. Martinez violated?

A. Americans with Disabilities Act
B. Fair Housing Act of 1968
C. Civil Rights Law of 1866
D. Fair Housing Amendments of 1988

Contract Law

1. An unenforceable contract

A. is one in which one party entered into the contract under duress.
B. is a void contract.
C. appears to meet the requirements of validity but would not be enforceable in court.
D. must involve a legal minor.

2. Revocation of the offer by the offeror prior to acceptance and its notification results in

A. termination.
B. acceptance.
C. postponement.
D. validation.

3. The following are relevant to an effective competitive market analysis EXCEPT

A. use of properties as similar as possible.
B. use of properties with most recent dates of sale.
C. listing broker identification.
D. use of minimum of three comparables.

4. Seller Louise signs a purchase agreement with buyer Tom, contingent upon a termite inspection. In this contract, seller Louise agrees that she will pay up to 2 percent of the purchase price for any repairs that a licensed termite inspector indicates must be done. Upon inspection, it is discovered that the repairs will exceed four percent of the purchase price. The purchase agreement is now

A. unenforceable.
B. voidable.
C. executed.
D. void.

5. Bill and Susan signed a contract to purchase an existing home last month, but they now have an opportunity to purchase a new construction home, which they initially preferred. Through negotiations with the sellers, the buyers are released from the contract to purchase the existing home by agreeing to forfeit their earnest money plus $5,000 to the sellers. This agreement is termed

A. operation of law.
B. complete performance.
C. accord and satisfaction.
D. novation.

6. Under which type of listing for sale is the broker assured a commission regardless of who sells the property during the listing term?

A. Exclusive agency
B. Open
C. Right of first refusal
D. Exclusive-right-to-sell

7. The Statute of Frauds requires that

A. all real estate contracts that involve the sale of an interest in land be in writing to be enforceable.
B. all contracts be in writing.
C. only real estate title transfer contracts be in writing.
D. all written real estate title transfer contracts use a certain form to be enforceable.

8. Scott will list his farm for sale with Tom Billings, a local broker who specializes in farm and land transactions. Scott will retain the right to sell the property himself, but assures Tom that he is the only broker Scott wants to work with. Tom advises Scott to sign a contract for a/an

A. exclusive-right-to-sell.
B. open listing.
C. nonexclusive agency.
D. exclusive agency.

9. An investor purchases a five-family house whose tenants hold current leases at the time of the closing. The new owner now has the right to collect the rents. This is an example of

A. specific performance.
B. accord and satisfaction.
C. novation.
D. assignment.

10. A contract whereby the buyer will occupy the property upon paying the purchase price in installments and the seller agrees to transfer title to the buyer upon receiving full payment from the buyer is called all of the following EXCEPT

A. contract for deed.
B. land contract.
C. option.
D. conditional sales contract.

11. All of the following statements are true EXCEPT

A. oral testimony alone is sufficient to enforce a contract for the transfer of real estate title.
B. parol evidence rule permits oral explanations in support of a written contract but not to contradict the terms of the contract.
C. the Statute of Frauds requires all real estate contracts be written and contain the essential elements for a valid contract.
D. a primary purpose of the Statute of Frauds is to state which contracts must be in writing to be enforceable.

12. Which statement is true regarding an option contract?

A. The optionor pays for the right to purchase by a specific date but does not promise to purchase
B. Because two parties agree, the option is a bilateral contract
C. The optionee promises to allow the optionor the sole right to purchase the property by a specific date
D. An option is an express unilateral contract

13. Which of the following is NOT a remedy for breach of contract?

A. Liquidated damages
B. Specific performance
C. Compensatory damages
D. Novation

14. A woman promises to hold 10 acres of her land to sell to her nephew within 10 months from today for $100,000. The nephew promises nothing in return. The legal agreement they both sign is

A. executed.
B. bilateral.
C. unenforceable.
D. an option.

15. Essential elements of a contract include all of the following EXCEPT

A. capacity of the parties.
B. value of comparable sales.
C. consideration.
D. legality of object.

16. When two parties to a contract have made promises to each other, the contract that exists is known as a/an

A. option contract.
B. bilateral contract.
C. unilateral contract.
D. void contract.

17. A buyer and seller enter into a purchase agreement. Three weeks prior to the closing, the seller finds out that the buyer is a psychologist. The seller decides to back out of the transaction because he doesn't believe that psychology is an honorable profession. The buyer wants the transaction to be completed and files a lawsuit for which of the following?

A. Specific performance
B. Actual damages
C. Rescission
D. Discrimination

18. "Specific performance" is based on all of the following statements EXCEPT

A. all legal contracts must be executed.
B. a contract will be completed as originally agreed.
C. each piece of real estate is unique.
D. there is no exact substitute for a piece of real estate.

19. All of the following are true of a land contract EXCEPT a land contract

A. provides equitable title to the buyer.
B. cannot be used on land purchases.
C. must be in writing to be enforceable.
D. is binding on the heirs and estates of the parties.

20. The two tests that entitle a broker to compensation are

A. buyer ready; seller acceptance.
B. buyer ready, willing, and able; seller acceptance.
C. buyer ready and willing; seller acceptance.
D. buyer financially capable; seller acceptance.

21. The term "meeting of the minds" is synonymous with what essential element of a contract?

A. Offer and acceptance
B. Competence
C. Legality of object
D. Consideration

22. An example of liquidated damages is

A. penalty for a party taking fraudulent advantage over another.
B. money actually lost.
C. penalty for extremely bad behavior by a party.
D. forfeiture of earnest money.

23. A listing contract creates a

A. contract for sale.
B. transfer of title.
C. license.
D. fiduciary-agency relationship.

24. In the event that a contract requires a court's interpretation, the court will first determine the

A. validity of the contract.
B. parties to the contract.
C. date of the contract.
D. length of the contract.

25. All of the following are essential elements of a contract EXCEPT

A. consideration.
B. legal capacity of the parties.
C. offer and acceptance.
D. date.

26. Listing contracts usually contain all of the following EXCEPT

A. commission rate or fee.
B. carryover clause.
C. beginning date and expiration date.
D. guarantee of sale.

27. A bilateral contract entered into by one party without full legal capacity is

A. enforceable.
B. void.
C. voidable.
D. valid.

28. An offer to buy may be terminated or concluded by all of the following EXCEPT

A. death or insanity prior to acceptance.
B. acceptance of the offer.

C. buyer remorse after offeror's acceptance.
D. rejection of the offer.

29. Under an exclusive-right-to-sell listing

A. if the seller finds his own buyer, he is relieved of paying the brokerage fee.
B. the broker employed has a right to a fee no matter who sells the property during the term of the listing.
C. the seller can expect that the company will not list any other properties like his until the house is sold.
D. the licensee exclusively represents the seller; all other licensees in the company represent the buyer.

30. At the time an offer is written, the broker tells the buyer the house is 2,300 square feet. The broker knows this is not true. After the seller accepts the buyer's offer, the buyer learns that the house is 2,100 square feet. At this point, the contract is considered

A. enforceable.
B. valid.
C. void.
D. voidable.

31. Which of the following is NOT an example of a means of legal discharge of a contract by operation of law?

A. Alteration of contract
B. Statute of limitations
C. Bankruptcy petition
D. Assignment of contract

32. The term "time is of the essence" in a contract means

A. the receipt for the acceptance of the offer was timed and dated.
B. the closing must take place within 10 days of all parties signing the contract.
C. all time frames in the contract must be strictly adhered to.
D. the contract must be performed within a statutory period of time.

33. An exclusive agency listing compensates the broker

A. when he shows the property for the principal.
B. upon presentation of an offer for the principal.
C. when he produces a buyer acceptable to the seller.
D. at the time of the listing.

34. A purchase agreement can be completed or terminated in all of the following situations EXCEPT when

A. most terms and conditions of the contract are met.
B. deadlines have expired and conditions were not met.
C. the property is destroyed by fire or flood.
D. all terms and conditions of the contract are met.

35. A contract is drawn to convey Lot Number 3 from Sunshine Developers, Inc. to Mr. Stevens. Upon further investigation, it is discovered that the lot selected by Stevens was Lot Number 4. Both parties recognize an error was made and agree to correct the contract. The error is an example of

A. misrepresentation.
B fraud.
C. mutual mistake.
D. legality of object.

36. A broker persuades his mother-in-law to purchase an overpriced property immediately to avoid the need of her moving into his home. This action could be interpreted as

A. duress.
B. fraud.
C. undue influence.
D. misrepresentation.

37. The contract relationship between the parties to an accepted offer to purchase is referred to as

A. fiduciary.
B. arm's length.
C. parol evidence.
D. agency.

38. A mature seventeen-year-old college student signs a contract to lease an apartment for one year with a one-year renewal clause. The lessor accepts the agreement. The validity of this contract may be in jeopardy due to

A. reality of consent.
B. offer and acceptance.
C. legal capacity of the parties.
D. consideration of the lease.

39. "The seller lists the property with several brokers" describes a/an

A. land contract.
B. open listing.
C. option.
D. exclusive-right-to-sell listing.

40. The broker's commission entitlement is tested by all of the following EXCEPT buyer is

A. able.
B. ready.
C. open to negotiation.
D. willing.

41. The purpose of earnest money includes all of the following EXCEPT to

A. help demonstrate the buyer's capability to raise sufficient funds to purchase the property.
B. show the sincerity of the buyer.
C. buy down the interest rate of the mortgage loan.
D. serve as liquidated damages to the seller in the event of the buyer's default.

42. The substitution of a new contract to replace a prior contract is a form of contract termination called

A. assignment.
B. full performance.
C. meeting of the minds.
D. novation.

43. The purpose of recording a land contract is to provide constructive notice for each of the following EXCEPT the

A. vendor's right to payment by the vendee.
B. vendor's legal title.
C. materialman's right to collect.
D. vendee's equitable title.

44. When the parties to a contract have definitely agreed to all terms and conditions in the contract, the type of contract that exists is known as

A. express.
B. implied.
C. promissory.
D. executed.

45. All of the following are circumstances that terminate a listing contract EXCEPT

A. destruction of the property.
B. renewal of the contract at expiration.
C. death or incapacity of the seller.
D. mutual agreement of the seller and the broker.

46. Which statement is NOT true about an accepted offer to purchase?

A. The parties are assumed to be in equal bargaining positions
B. The principals have formed an agency relationship with each other
C. The purchase contract is a bilateral express contract
D. The parties have equal ability from opposing viewpoints

47. A contract that is binding and enforceable on all parties to it is known as

A. voidable.
B. valid.
C. void.
D. executed.

48. What is the broker's prime obligation in a listing contract?

A. To advertise the property
B. To obtain any buyer
C. To use his "best effort" to achieve the sale of the property
D. To generate income and preserve value of the property

49. The rights, duties, and responsibilities of the parties are wholly expressed through the

A. contract.
B. application.
C. acceptance.
D. offer.

50. In selecting comparable properties for a competitive market analysis, it is essential to select

A. similar properties in adjacent communities.
B. the highest valued properties in the area.
C. similar properties in the neighborhood
D. the average of the highest and lowest valued properties in the neighborhood

Transfers of Title

1. Which deed places grantor Deborah in a position with the LEAST liability to grantee Terry?

A. Quitclaim deed
B. Bargain and sale deed
C. General Warranty deed
D. Special Warranty deed

2. Fleming has died leaving a fairly sizable estate and a complicated will. A court action has been filed to test the validity of the will. The process is called

A. descent.
B. probate.
C. distribution.
D. execution of the will.

3. Who has the right to name the executor of an estate?

A. Devisee
B. Testator
C. Trustee
D. Personal representative

4. The person who gives the title by deed in a real estate transaction is the

A. devisor.
B. devisee.
C. grantee.
D. grantor.

5. Jackson has bought a new home and received a deed. Jackson's recording of this deed provides

A. constructive notice effective against any subsequent claims.
B. protection against any previous liens or claims.
C. actual transfer of the deed.
D. proof of free and clear title for Jackson.

6. A complete examination of title typically involves

A. researching the public record from the present back in time.
B. examination of the property.
C. verifying only the last transfer of property.
D. a survey.

7. As the executor of her mother's estate, Harriman would sign which type of deed to sell the estate's real property?

A. Quitclaim deed
B. Deed of trust
C. Special warranty deed
D. General warranty deed

8. The S ½ of the NE ¼ of the NE ¼ of section 26, T3N, R6E contains how many acres?

A. 10
B. 40
C. 80
D. 20

9. The purpose of acknowledgement of a deed is to verify the

A. receipt of the deed by the grantee.
B. correct preparation of the deed.
C. quality of title being transferred.
D. intent of the grantor and make the deed eligible for recording.

10. Buyer Madden would gain the greatest protection from which type of deed when purchasing property?

A. Quitclaim deed
B. General warranty deed
C. Special warranty deed
D. Bargain and sale deed

11. A metes and bounds description of land must

A. measure all references with precise angles and distances.
B. identify only parcels with straight property lines and not curved lines.
C. be approved by the U.S. government survey system.
D. begin and end at the same point.

12. Among the essential elements of a deed is

A. the signature of the grantee.
B. covenant of seisin and right to convey.
C. it must be in writing.
D. recording.

13. The number of square feet in an acre is

A. 5,280.
B. 43,560.
C. 160.
D. 43,650.

14. Marketable title of property means

A. free and clear of all liens.
B. that title can readily be resold or mortgaged.
C. the property is listed at a reasonable price.
D. a title policy has been ordered.

15. Donoher's deed contains a covenant against encumbrances, a covenant of quiet enjoyment, and a covenant of further assurance among others. Donoher's deed is a

A. deed of trust.
B. quitclaim deed.
C. general warranty deed.
D. bargain and sale deed.

16. A father transfers a piece of property to his daughter by means of quitclaim deed. The daughter places the deed in a safety deposit box. This deed is

A. voidable.
B. invalid.
C. void.
D. valid.

17. Which of these descriptive references is NOT relevant for a metes and bounds type description?

A. Plat
B. Degree
C. Point of beginning
D. Monument

18. A transfer of personal property during one's lifetime is shown by a bill of sale. The equivalent document to transfer real property is a/an

A. deed.
B. will.
C. abtract of title.
D. affidavit.

19. A lien foreclosure sale, title transfer may occur by all of the following EXCEPT

A. trustee's deed.
B. involuntary alienation.
C. voluntary alienation.
D. sheriff's deed.

20. Bakeman's property is being sold. Buyer Svoboda has asked for proof of title through a summary of the property's title history and has asked his attorney to review this history. This summary is called a/an

A. owner's title insurance policy.
B. abstract.
C. opinion.
D. deed.

21. Three years after purchasing a piece of property, a buyer is notified by the son of the property owner from 15 years ago that his father never signed the deed when the property was sold. The son is claiming an interest to the property. His claim will be handled by the

A. person who purchased the property from the son's father.
B. title insurance company that insured the title.
C. criminal courts because the transfer is illegal.
D. current owner.

22. Personal property transferred at death is called a legacy. Real property transferred at death is called a/an

A. bequest.
B. devise.
C. inheritance.
D. gift.

23. A plat would best be described as a

A. metes and bounds.
B. deed.
C. map.
D. legal description.

24. How many acres are there in a section?

A. 43,560
B.   36
C.   640
D.   6

25. The history of ownership of real property showing each owner of the property in the past is referred to as

A. chain of title.
B. opinion of title.
C. marketable title.
D. title insurance.

76

26. The term "intestate" means a

A. deceased person has insufficient assets to cover her debts.
B. person has died with no valid will.
C. person has died and all of her property is located in the state in which the decedent resided.
D. deceased person's assets will all pass to the state.

27. Corcos is buying a home. He is concerned about the quality of title. Which of these is NOT a method of inspecting and assuring that Corcos will have marketable title?

A. Abstract and opinion
B. Title examination
C. Recording his deed
D. Title insurance

28. In order for Johnson to claim ownership of Green's land under adverse possession, she must show all of the following EXCEPT

A. open and notorious use.
B. exclusive use apart from Green.
C. permission of Green.
D. continuous possession.

29. A person who buys property by relying on the records and is unaware of any unrecorded prior documents is a

A. land contract vendor.
B. bona fide purchaser.
C. grantor.
D. mortgagee.

30. Which of the following parties to a deed does NOT have to have legal capacity as an absolute requirement?

A. Corporate grantor

B. Grantor
C. Grantee
D. Notary public

31. Which deed would be used by a grantor who has a claim of title and possession in the property because he was the successful bidder at a foreclosure sale?

A. Sheriff's deed
B. Deed of trust
C. Special warranty deed
D. Quitclaim deed

32. The policy that insures the lender against defects in the title is which of the following?

A. Borrower's policy
B. Owner's policy
C. Homeowner's policy
D. Mortgage's policy

33. Miguel Fernandez has died and named his sister, Lupe, to handle the affairs of his estate until all real and personal property are distributed to Lupe and her husband, Manuel. Which word would NOT properly describe Lupe's role?

A. Testatrix
B. Devisee
C. Beneficiary
D. Probate

34. Under the government survey system the notation R17E would be east of a

A. township.
B. range.
C. baseline.
D. principal meridian.

35. The recipient of title by delivery of a valid deed is always a

A. vendor.
B. grantor.
C. grantee.
D. vendee.

36. The final step to effect the transfer of title by deed is

A. recording the deed.
B. signing by the grantor.
C. acknowledgement before a notary.
D. delivery to and acceptance by the grantee.

37. Which term is most closely associated with descent?

A. Testator
B. Devise
C. Voluntary alienation
D. Personal representative

38. Which of the following is true regarding property descriptions?

A. A street address takes precedence over a legal description.
B. The assessor's parcel number is the only legal description necessary for recordation.
C. If a lot, block, and subdivision plat reference is used along with a street address that does not identify the same property, the street address takes precedence.
D. Metes and bounds descriptions are valid legal descriptions for a recorded document.

39. The transfer of title to real property from seller Johnson to buyer Trang is called

A. habendum.
B. probate.
C. subrogation.
D. alienation.

40. The NE ¼ of the NW ¼ of section 21, T4S, R11E is a description of land by

A. metes and bounds.
B. reference.
C. U.S. Rectangular Survey System.
D. plat map.

41. As Wilson buys her home she insists upon proof of title with financial protection against certain defects in title. Wilson is demanding

A. title insurance.
B. a contract buyer's policy.
C. homeowner's insurance.
D. an abstract of title and attorney's opinion.

42. A description by reference

A. makes reference to other documents in the possession of the grantor.
B. refers to previously recorded documents such as a deed or plat map.
C. always references the area of the parcel.
D. outlines all points of reference, corners, and angles in the wording or the description.

43. Bernstein has just bought a home for $125,000 with a $20,000 down payment. A title insurance policy has been issued for $105,000. This title policy would be a/an

A. contract buyer's policy.
B. owner's policy.
C. leasehold policy.
D. mortgagee's policy.

44. A township contains

A. 640 acres.
B. plat.
C. 36 square miles.
D. one section.

45. Which of the following transfers of title is voluntary during one's lifetime?

A. Devise
B. Adverse possession
C. Eminent domain
D. Conveyance by deed

46. A property sells for $158,000. Which of the following is the amount of revenue stamps the seller will be responsible for at closing?

A. $1,324.40
B. $ 679.40
C. $ 1,264
D. $1,358.80

Real Estate Finance

1. When a payment is made on an amortizing loan, what is the payment applied to last?

A. Principal

B. Interest
C. Insurance
D. Taxes

2. The lender on Johnson's mortgage has elected to force Johnson to pay off his mortgage rather than let a new buyer assume that loan. This is the lender's right under the

A. assumption clause.
B. alienation clause.
C. acceleration clause.
D. reconveyance clause.

3. The LEAST likely type of foreclosure in the United States is

A. strict.
B. non-judicial.
C. statutory.
D. judicial.

4. A lender may acquire title after a default by the borrower in all of the following situations. Which one of these would NOT eliminate any junior liens?

A. Non-judicial foreclosure
B. Strict foreclosure
C. Deed in lieu of foreclosure
D. Judicial foreclosure

5. Thompson is several months behind in her payments. The lender is starting foreclosure proceedings with the full balance due immediately. This is the lender's right according to the

A. defeasance clause.
B. acceleration clause.
C. granting clause.
D. alienation clause.

6. The Michigan Due on Sale Clause Act applies to

A. only VA-guaranteed loans.
B. loans made by state-chartered lenders.
C. all real estate loans.
D. only FHA-insured loans.

7. The amount of money that is advanced by the lender and ultimately repaid by the borrower is referred to as

A. interest.
B. note.
C. principal.
D. mortgage.

8. The amount of an assumed mortgage would appear on the seller's statement as a

A. liability.
B. disbursement.
C. debit.
D. credit.

9. All the following are true EXCEPT

A. VA insures repayment of the top portion of a loan to the lender in the event of a default.
B. VA-guaranteed loan can be 100 percent loan.
C. VA loans are for owner-occupied homes.
D. the loan amount is based on the lesser of the certificate of reasonable value (CRV) or the purchase price.

10. A purchase money mortgage may be

A. guaranteed by VA.
B. insured by FHA.
C. a land contract.
D. a first mortgage.

11. Which of the following is NOT required in a mortgage or deed of trust?

A. It must contain a mortgaging clause or statement of intent to mortgage
B. It must describe the property
C. The borrower must have a free and clear title
D. It must be in writing

12. The lender in a deed of trust is also the

A. beneficiary.
B. mortgagor.
C. trustee.
D. trustor.

13. The secondary mortgage market provides which of the following to mortgages and their lenders?

A. Liquidity
B. Assignment
C. Lower interest rates
D. Disintermediation

14. If an assumption of an existing loan takes place and the original borrower is relieved of liability, this is referred to as a/an

A. defeasance.
B. novation.
C. redemption.
D. alienation.

15. The most common way to purchase real property is

A. a cash purchase.
B. through an assumption.
C. with a VA loan.
D. with new financing.

16. Ruiz has obtained a new loan on his home. Two months later the lender notifies Ruiz that future payments should be made to Central States Mortgage Co. The original mortgagee has executed its right of

A. assignment.
B. acceleration.
C. novation.
D. assumption.

17. The document that shows that a debt exists and how it will be repaid is the

A. mortgage.
B. deed of trust.
C. promissory note.
D. sales contract.

18. Michigan law grants a borrower the right to redeem property after a foreclosure sale has occurred. This right of redemption is referred to as

A. equitable.
B. strict.
C. statutory.
D. non-recourse.

19. If Mitchell allows Thompson to assume her loan and Thompson defaults in the payments, is Mitchell still liable on the loan?

A. No, because Thompson assumed all liability
B. Yes, unless Mitchell has been released from liability
C. Yes, because Mitchell is liable until it is paid off
D. No, as long as Thompson had to qualify for the assumption

20. If the sales proceeds are insufficient to pay all of the costs of the foreclosure and the secured liens, the borrower may still be held responsible for any remaining shortage under which of the following?

A. Deficiency judgment
B. Right of assignment
C. Strict foreclosures
D. Redemptive right

21. Which of these organizations would NOT be a likely purchaser of a recently originated mortgage loan?

A. FNMA
B. GNMA
C. REIT
D. FHLMC

22. All of the following are true regarding a purchaser qualifying for a loan under the Michigan State Housing Development Act, MSHDA, EXCEPT

A. the interest rate will be lower than other loans.
B. the home may be a new construction
C. the home may be used only as a principal residence.
D. there are no income limit qualifications.

23. When a lien is paid off, the lien should be removed as a cloud on the title. This removal of a lien usually is called

A. release.
B. novation.
C. assumption.
D. encumbrance.

24. Williams is paying off his loan 18 years early to refinance to a lower interest rate. His current lender is asking for a 1 point fee in addition to the balance due. This is a/an:

A. prepayment penalty.
B. defeasance fee.
C. discount point.
D. acceleration penalty.

25. Under the Michigan Mortgage Brokers, Lenders, and Servicers Licensing Act, any person who, directly or indirectly, serves or offers to serve as an agent for any person in an attempt to obtain a mortgage loan is a mortgage

A. servicer.
B. lender.
C. banker.
D. broker.

26. Baxter has borrowed $40,000 against his home with a second mortgage from Ace Mortgage Company. In this transaction, Ace Mortgage Company is

A. beneficiary.
B. mortgage.
C. trustor.
D. mortgagor.

27. Which secondary mortgage organization is the most recently created and specializes in the purchase and sale of conventional loans in the secondary market?

A. MGIC
B. FHLMC
C. GNMA
D. FNMA

28. A property has three liens encumbering it: a first mortgage, a second mortgage, and a third mortgage. These numbers refer to

A. the dates of the liens.
B. the size of the liens.
C. whether the liens are from a seller, a mortgage company, or a third-party lender.
D. the priority of the liens.

29. The best word to describe the action of financing property is

A. borrowing.
B. note.
C. interest.
D. mortgage.

30. A mortgage is

A. note.
B. security instrument.
C. defeasance.
D. loan.

31. Power of sale is most closely associated with

A. judicial foreclosure.
B. non-judicial foreclosure.
C. strict foreclosure.
D. equitable redemption.

32. A mortgage clause that allows the borrower to force the release of the lien when the debt is paid in full is a/an

A. alienation clause.
B. habendum clause.
C. defeasance clause.
D. acceleration clause.

33. Someone who brings a lender and a borrower together for a fee paid by the lender is a

A. credit union.
B. mortgage broker.
C. savings banks.
D. real estate investment trust.

34. A three-party financing arrangement in which title is transferred to a disinterested third party would be

A. deed of trust.
B. option.
C. mortgage.
D. land contract.

35. When depositors remove their funds from banks, savings and loans, and other lending institutions to invest elsewhere for a higher yield, it is referred to as

A. assignment.
B. liquidation.
C. disintermediation.
D. defeasance.

36. Marta has pledged her home and a neighboring parcel as blanket security for a note but still retains possession of both. This pledging is an example of

A. liquidity.
B. a deed of trust.
C. hypothecation.
D. a mortgage.

37. Michigan's Mortgage Brokers, Lenders, and Servicers Licensing Act covers all of the following EXCEPT

A. duplexes located in Michigan.
B. loans for one-to-four-family residential properties.
C. land contracts.

D. vacant land.

38. The secondary mortgage market is

A. regulated by state law.
B. where mortgages are brought sold after they have been originated.
C. where a borrower who has poor credit may seek a loan.
D. where one might obtain a second mortgage.

39. Which of the following is true regarding recording a mortgage document?

A. An unrecorded mortgage is illegal
B. Mortgages must be recorded to be valid
C. Mortgages must be recorded to effectively provide notice
D. The priority of mortgages is established by the date of each mortgage

40. The major difference between judicial and non-judicial foreclosure is that judicial foreclosure

A. requires advertisement of the public sale; non-judicial requires no advertisement.
B. is faster than non-judicial.
C. requires a power of sale clause in the mortgage; non-judicial does not.
D. involves court proceeding non-judicial is the power of sale bypassing court action.

41. Tennyson is several months behind in his mortgage payments. The mortgage company has begun foreclosure, with the sale scheduled for three weeks from today. Tennyson has just received an inheritance large enough to pay off the debt, interest, and costs. If he does pay it

off, he will have done so under which of the following?

A. Acceleration
B. Power of sale
C. Reinstatement
D. Equitable redemption

42. Which secondary mortgage organization is an agency of the federal government limited to purchasing FHA and VA loans?

A. FNMA
B. FHLMC
C. GNMA
D. MGIC

43. In order for loans to be eligible for purchase by FNMA and FHLMC, they must meet certain standards regarding qualification, appraisal, and contract terms. Loans that meet those standards and are eligible are referred to as

A. conforming loans.
B. amortizing loans.
C. conventional loans.
D. land contract loans.

Real Estate Appraisal

1. Which of the following is a correct application of the capitalization formula?

A. Gross rent X gross rent multiplier = value
B. Annual net income divided by capitalization rate = value
C. Gross income divided by capitalization rate = value
D. Value X capitalization rate = effective gross income

2. Carole Kowalski purchased a home with a one-car garage. This is an example of which of the following?

A. Assessed obsolescence
B. Functional obsolescence
C. Physical deterioration
D. Economic obsolescence

3. Under Michigan law, limited real estate appraisers may perform only appraisals

A. not involving federally related transactions.
B. properties where the specialist is acting as an agent.
C. where the appraiser receives a fee from the lender.
D. one-to-four-family property residential loans.

4. Which appraised property would be LEAST suited to the income approach?

A. Mini-storage units
B. Single-family rental home
C. Vacant downtown land
D. Apartment building

5. The most appropriate appraisal approach in appraising single-family homes and vacant land is

A. building residual technique.
B. cost approach.
C. market data.
D. income approach.

6. A property does not show well due to old, yellowed wallpaper and faded paint in several rooms. This is an example of

A. regression.
B. functional obsolescence.
C. change.
D. physical deterioration.

7. The fact that a property has the ability to satisfy a need in the marketplace is referred to as

A. effective demand.
B. utility.
C. transferability.
D. scarcity.

8. A key point in the estimate of market value is that the appraiser should be

A. investing in similar properties himself.
B. an active real estate broker.
C. objective in his or her approach.
D. willing to invest in the property if value is high enough.

9. To determine the reproduction cost of a structure with the greatest precision one would use the

A. unit-in-place method.
B. cubic foot method.
C. square foot method.
D. quantity survey method.

10. Land use studies, highest and best use, and marketability studies are all examples of

A. assessed value.
B. evaluation.
C. book value.
D. valuation.

11. Which property would be best appraised by the cost approach?

A. Apartment building
B. Land
C. Single-family home
D. A not-for-profit hospital

12. Which type of depreciation is always incurable?

A. Economic obsolescence
B. Physical deterioration
C. Diminishing returns
D. Functional obsolescence

13. Which type of value would be most relevant to a city or county budget official?

A. Condemnation value
B. Book value
C. Assessed value
D. Insurance value

14. Which type of value would be most important to a residential real estate salesperson?

A. Assessed value
B. Condemnation value
C. Hazard insurance value
D. Mortgage loan value

15. The greater the risk to an investor, the greater the

A. potential rate of return.
B. gross rent multiplier.
C. investment.
D. value.

16. The difference between valuation and evaluation is

A. evaluation requires a license; valuation does not.
B. valuation is the determination of the probable price; evaluation does not result in an estimate of property value.
C. valuation is the same as a CMA; evaluation is a formal appraisal.
D. evaluation provides a legal value.

17. There is a tremendous shortage of housing in the area but interest rates are 16%. Despite the many prospective buyers, very few can qualify at these rates. The problem in this market is a lack of

A. utility.
B. transferability.
C. effective demand.
D. scarcity.

18. If property is being claimed by a local government for location of a new freeway, the relevant value is

A. book value.
B. insurance value.
C. assessed value.
D. condemnation value.

19. The highest and best use of a property is

A. only the use to which it is being put presently.
B. only for residential use.
C. the feasible use that will produce the highest present value.
D. the use that most densely utilizes the property.

20. Both the cost approach and the sales comparison approach in appraisal are

based heavily on what the buyer would have to pay for an equally useful and desirable alternative. This is the principle of

A. conformity.
B. substitution.
C. highest and best use.
D. contribution.

21. A decline in value from any cause is

A. regression.
B. functional obsolescence.
C. deterioration.
D. depreciation.

22. A property has recently been appraised. The value derived is

A. book value.
B. the legal value.
C. an estimate.
D. the lowest amount a seller will accept.

23. The acronym DUST stands for:

A. Demand, utility, scarcity, transferability
B. Depreciation, under improvement, substitution, tacking
C. Demand, usage, salability, title
D. Demographics, utility, scarcity, transferability

24. Although an appraisal and a competitive market analysis (CMA) employ many similar principles, they are different. One of these major differences is

A. performing a CMA requires an appraisal license; an appraisal does not.
B. a CMA does not examine sold properties; an appraisal does.
C. an appraisal is required for loans funded by or insured by the government, but a CMA is not.
D. a CMA is a special type of appraisal on income property only.

25. An appraiser is comparing two homes that sold in the last 60 days. The only major difference is that one had a fireplace and the other did not. The one with the fireplace sold for $1,100 more. The value of the fireplace is based on the principle of

A. conformity.
B. substitution.
C. anticipation.
D. contribution.

26. The most comprehensive appraisal report is

A. the Uniform Residential Appraisal Report (URAR).
B. the market data approach.
C. a Certificate of Reasonable Value.
D. a narrative appraisal.

27. An older home has workable plumbing handles that all come directly out of the wall with separate spouts for hot and cold, as opposed to the more modern faucets coming out of the sink top. This is an example of
A. anticipation.

B. physical deterioration.
C. functional obsolescence.
D. economic obsolescence.

28. Changes to an area due to future growth patterns, traffic routing, and specific development plans can all affect the value of property. This is the principle of

A. anticipation.
B. conformity.
C. progression.
D. regression.

29. Which of the following is NOT included in determining market value?

A. Payment should be in cash or readily available financing
B. The seller must want to sell very quickly, at all costs
C. Buyer and seller should be equally motivated
D. Both buyer and seller should be knowledgeable about the property

30. Which of the following factors is NOT a valid criterion for assessing value?

A. Racial composition of the area
B. Economic factors of the local area
C Physical factors of the land and improvement
D. Governmental factors such as zoning and taxation

31. The act performing routine maintenance and improvements will effect on the

A. functional obsolescence.
B. effective age.
C. economic obsolescence.
D. actual age.

32. Which application would most likely be used in a cost approach appraisal for a 200-year-old building?

A. Reproduction cost
B. Quantity survey method
C. Replacement cost
D. Cubic foot method

33. An added investment in property that does not yield a return to the owner is

A. functional advantage.
B. economic advantage.
C. under-improvement.
D. over-improvement.

34. The economic principles of supply and demand are best shown in the characteristic of

A. effective demand.
B. transferability.
C. scarcity.
D. utility.

35. The major difference between gross rent multiplier (GRM) and the capitalization rate is the multiplier

A. can be applied only to residential property; the cap rate can be applied to any income property.
B. is based on monthly figures; the cap rate is based on yearly figures.
C. deals with gross income and does not account for vacancies or expenses; the cap rate deals with net income.
D. varies; the cap rate is fixed.

36. In Michigan a licensee who wishes to do appraisals and act as a real estate practitioner MUST

A. be sponsored by a state-certified appraiser who also has a broker's license.
B. obtain licenses in accordance with Michigan's appraisal law and real estate license law.
C. obtain permission of the employing broker.
D. do appraisals only on property listed by the licensee

37. Land is NOT included in calculating which value?

A. Hazard insurance value
B. Condemnation value
C. Book value
D. Assessed value

38. Which type of value is most relevant for the preparation of income taxes?

A. Insurance value
B. Mortgage loan value
C. Assessed value
D. Book value

39. Jennings has a property upon which he has sold a three-year option. The option has not yet been exercised and has a year until expiration. The property has risen in value dramatically above the option price in the last six months. Jennings' position is hurt by the lack of

A. effective demand.
B. utility.
C. transferability.
D. scarcity.

Land Use Controls

1. Which of the following is exempt from compliance with the Interstate Land Sales Full Disclosure Act?

A. A subdivision of 30 one-acre lots
B. Lots offered exclusively to the elderly
C. A subdivision with 35 seven-acre lots
D. Lots with utilities established

2. Developers offering 25 or more lots across state lines must provide a property report to the prospective buyer and a statement of record to HUD according to

A. the National Environmental Policy Act of 1969.
B. local building codes.
C. the Interstate Land Sales Full Disclosure Act.
D. the Truth-in-Lending Act.

3. Limitations placed on the use of land by the developer of a residential subdivision are known as

A. restrictive covenants.
B. planned unit development.
C. SARA.
D. variances.

4. The legal basis for cities and counties to develop long-range plans for growth are

A. zoning ordinances.
B. enabling acts.
C. restrictive covenants.
D. variances.

5. Violations of zoning laws can result in any of the following measures EXCEPT

A. correction by demolishing an unlawful structure.
B. enforcement by fines.
C. correction by court action.
D. suit to quiet title.

6. Specific regulations governing the materials used in construction, fire and safety standards, and sanitary equipment facilities are referred to as

A. deed restrictions.
B. zoning ordinances.
C. restrictive covenants.
D. building codes.

7. The 1986 act that imposed more stringent clean up standards for hazardous sites and expanded the definition of persons liable for the cost of clean up is known as

A. the Environmental Policy Act.
B. CERCLA.
C. SARA.
D. TSCA.

8. When ownership of a property is being transferred, mandatory city certification allows a city government to inspect the property in all the following areas EXCEPT

A. number of current occupants.
B. plumbing.
C. electrical system.
D. roofing.

9. Private land use controls are enforced by public law through a court order known as a/an

A. injunction.
B. judgment.
C. writ of execution.
D. attachment.

10. If spot zoning of a property is solely for the benefit of the property owner and has the effect of increasing the land value, the rezoning is

A. referred to as a "variance."
B. referred to as a "nonconforming use."
C. legal.
D. illegal and invalid.

11. The Interstate Land Sales Full Disclosure Act regulates developers of subdivisions of 25 or

A. more lots offered within state lines.
B. fewer lots offered across state lines.
C. more lots offered across state lines.
D. fewer lots offered within state lines.

12. All of the following are privately imposed land use controls EXCEPT

A. condition.
B. covenant.
C. variance.
D. deed restriction.

13. Which of the following does NOT describe typical planning and zoning?

A. Planning and zoning that results in social and economic benefits to the community
B. Planning and zoning that requires the unanimous consent of all property owners within a community
C. Planning and zoning that are based on the police power of government
D. Planning and zoning that provides for the orderly growth of a community.

14. The document that permits occupancy of a structure by the tenants or the owner is called a/an

A. declaration of restrictions.
B. property report.
C. enabling act.
D. certificate of occupancy.

15. Which of the following does NOT refer to a type of zoning established by a zoning map?

A. Cluster
B. Residential
C. Spot
D. Multiple use

16. The primary purpose of subdivision regulations is to protect purchasers and taxpayers in the community against

A. racial integration among residents.
B. zoning.
C. undue taxes required for additional services.
D. enabling acts.

17. All of the following statements are true regarding restrictive covenants EXCEPT

A. failing to enforce restrictions in a timely manner may result in loss of the right to enforce them at all.
B. an injunction prevents a use contrary to the restrictions of record.
C. enforcement of covenants is limited to the original purchasers.
D. private land use control is enforced by public law.

18. According to Michigan's Wetland Protection Act, a person can do all of the following in a designated wetland without a permit EXCEPT

A. hike.
B. swim.
C. boat.
D. dredge.

19. Which of the following statements is NOT true about CERCLA?

A. It provides solutions to environmental problems
B. It funds clean up of hazardous sites
C. It defines hazardous substances
D. It identifies sites containing hazardous substances

20. Which of the following is a permitted deviation from the specific requirements of a zoning ordinance?

A. Encroachment
B. Certification of occupancy
C. Variance
D. Easement

21. All of the following statements are true when a subdivision is built in a zoned area EXCEPT

A. restrictive covenants can be implemented regardless of zoning ordinances.
B. restrictive covenants that are more restrictive than the zoning ordinance have priority over the zoning requirements.
C. if restrictive covenants are contrary to public law and policy, they will not be enforceable.
D. restrictive covenants are not valid until they are recorded properly on public records.

22. If a subdivision is in a zoned area, the subdivision's recorded restrictive covenants

A. have priority over the zoning ordinances if the covenants are less restrictive.
B. have priority over the zoning ordinances if the covenants are more restrictive.
C. may be contrary to the zoning ordinances.
D. must read precisely like the zoning Law.

23. Zoning ordinances consist of which two parts?

A. Planned unit developments and the zoning map
B. Cluster zoning and planned unit developments
C. Nonconforming use and spot zoning
D. The zoning map and the text of the zoning ordinance

24. Zoning laws that govern the distance between property lines and structures are known as

A. restrictive covenants.
B. right of ways.
C. setbacks.
D. enabling acts.

25. "A permitted deviation from specific requirements of the zoning ordinance" defines

A. subdivision regulations.
B. a planned unit development (PUD)
C. nonconforming use.
D. variance.

Encumbrances and Government Restrictions

1. If a real estate broker is in possession of keys to a seller's house, the broker is responsible for any loss or damage because he has

A. the right of ingress and egress.
B. created a bailment.
C. a use and occupancy permit.
D. a license from the seller.

2. The gradual build up of land in a watercourse over time by deposits of silt, sand, and gravel is called

A. avulsion.
B. littoral.
C. accession.
D. accretion.

3. If a state takes property under its power of escheat, it is because the property owner died

A. testate.
B. bankrupt.
C. intestate.
D. profit a prendre.

4. One of the current purposes of restrictive covenants is to

A. create a general use lien
B. maximize land values by requiring homogeneous use of land.
C. establish setback requirements.
D. legally prevent minorities from moving in.

5. When an owner is landlocked and has no access to roads, the landowner may go to court and ask for

A. easement by grant.
B. easement by condemnation.
C. easement by necessity.
D. encroachment.

6. Property owner A and property owner B have adjoining residential properties. Property owner B has permission from property owner A to use property owner A's driveway. Property B would be described as which of the following

A. dominant tenement.
B. easement in gross.
C. appurtenant easement.
D. servient tenement.

7. Proof of the existence or lack of existence of an encroachment is BEST evidenced by a

A. building permit.
B. deed.
C. survey.
D. profit.

8. Property owner Sam gives Jack temporary permission to fish off of his dock for one day. Jack's privilege exists in the form of which of the following

A. life estates.
B. license.
C. estate for years.
D. easement.

9. If property owner Mendoza sells his property, including an easement appurtenant, to property owner Hopkins, the easement is said to

A. run with the land.
B. create an additional easement in gross.
C. create an additional easement by implication.
D. create an additional easement by prescription.

10. The government's right to private property that is left by a person who has no heirs and no will is

A. eminent domain.
B. estate in remainder.
C. escheat.
D. police power.

11. In a lawsuit, Judy wins a judgment against Doris and all of Doris' property. This type of lien is known as

A. general lien.
B. mortgage lien.
C. mechanic's lien.
D. specific lien.

12. Compensation often follows a court action related to which of the following?

A. Restrictive covenants
B. Police power
C. Condemnation
D. Zoning

13. The difference between police power and eminent domain can best be determined by whether

A. the improvements are to be destroyed.
B. the owner's use was affected.
C. the action was by a governmental

agency.
D. any compensation was paid to an affected owner.

14. The term "appurtenances" refers to

A. automatic rights that are a natural consequence of owning property.
B. the right to take products of the soil from the land of another.
C. permission to do a particular act or a series of acts on the land of another without possession.
D. the reversion of an intestate decedent's property to the state.

15. A governmental power through which title to property reverts to the state when heirs to the property cannot be located is known as

A. escheat.
B. condemnation.
C. taxation.
D. encroachment.

16. Mechanic's liens usually receive preferential treatment because of

A. the type of documentation required to record.
B. the amount of the lien.
C. the penalties assessed if they are not paid.
D. their special priority.

17. Most road widening, sidewalk, alley, and utility easements are created with easements by

A. necessity.
B. condemnation.
C. prescription.
D. a grant.

18. Under the Michigan Construction Lien Act, the notice given to all subcontractors, materialmen, and laborers informing them where the work will be done is

A. waiver of lien.
B. notice of furnishing.
C. sworn statement.
D. notice of commencement.

19. Which of the following is NOT a specific lien?

A. Income tax
B. Real property tax
C. Mechanic's
D. Mortgage

20. No contract exists between New York City and Rockefeller Center. Every Christmas Day, the owners of Rockefeller Center close access to the center's sidewalks by setting up barriers on the sidewalks surrounding the building. This is done to prevent a claim by the city of New York based on easement by

A. prescription.
B. encroachment.
C. grant.
D. necessity.

21. Eminent domain is characterized by what limitation(s)?

A. The condemned property must be for the use and benefit of the general public.
B. Property owners must be paid the fair market value of the property lost plus any investment dollars expended.
C. The property owner must agree to the taking of the property.

D. It can only be exercised in times of a national emergency.

22. Property owner John gives his neighbor Maria the right to use his driveway to reach her garage. Maria's interest or right is called a/an

A. implied easement.
B. easement.
C. encroachment.
D. sublease.

23. An easement can be

A. eliminated without notice.
B. assigned.
C. granted by subdivision laws.
D. created by law, by use, or by humans.

24. Profit a prendre is

A. license.
B. right.
C. bailment.
D. leasehold.

25. Which of the following is NOT a government restriction on real property?

A. Restrictive covenant
B. Taxation
C. Eminent domain
D. Police power

26. The assessed value of properties in most areas of Michigan will equal

A. a total of the value of the land and buildings.
B. 50 percent of the market value.
C. twice the tax dollar amount.
D. 60 percent of the market value unless otherwise stated.

27. All of the following are encumbrances. Which one is not a lien as well?

A. Mortgage
B. Attachment
C. Property taxes
D. Deed restriction

28. A notice warning a prospective property purchaser that a lawsuit is commencing that could result in a recorded judgment that would create a lien against the property is a/an

A. restrictive covenant.
B. judgment.
C. attachment.
D. lis pendens.

29. Michigan requires construction liens to be filed in the county where the property is located within a specified number of days after furnishing labor or materials. That number of days is

A. 90 days.
B. 360 days.
C. 180 days.
D. 60 days.

30. The city of Palmcrest has placed liens on the properties located in Sunny Shores subdivision for the installation of streetlights. These liens are known as

A. special assessments.
B. general liens.
C. materialmen's liens.
D. tax assessments.

31. Which of the following is NOT a common appurtenant right?

A. Condemnation

B. Air rights
C. License
D. Profit a prendre

32. Landowners in Peyton Place subdivision are not allowed to paint their homes any color other than white and may only have tile roofs. This type of private restriction is known as a/an

A. condemnation.
B. trespass.
C. encroachment.
D. restrictive covenant.

33. Land that borders a river most likely would be governed by what type of water rights?

A. Littoral
B. Remainder
C. Reversion
D. Riparian

34. Developer Debbie sets aside a portion of the platted land in the new subdivision for parks and other common areas. This practice is called

A. dedication.
B. an easement by condemnation.
C. an easement by prescription.
D. an easement by necessity.

35. Mr. Bischler owns a piece of property that has a canal running through the back portion. He has ownership rights to the center of the canal according to which of the following

A. easement appurtenant.
B. writ of attachment.
C. littoral rights.
D. riparian rights.

Leasehold Estates

1. The consideration paid to the landlord is

A. rent.
B. recording.
C. privity of contract.
D. always for a fixed period of time.

2. A leasehold in which the term automatically renews unless proper notice is given is an

A. estate from year to year.
B. estate at will.
C. estate at sufferance.
D. estate for years.

3. The major purpose of a security deposit is to

A. collect the last month's rent before the tenant vacates.
B. ensure the return of the property in good repair.
C. prove the tenant's creditworthiness.
D. provide for routine maintenance.

4. The party transferring the right to possession under a lease is the

A. lessee.
B. lessor.
C. vendor.
D. tenant.

5. Jenkins has a lease that requires NO notice to terminate upon expiration of the initial term. Jenkins has an

A. estate at will.
B. estate from year to year.
C. estate at sufferance.
D. estate for years.

6. Which of these leases does NOT address future rent increases?

A. Gross
B. Graduated
C. Index
D. Escalated

7. Barring any wording in the lease to the contrary, the tenant may

A. not assign the leasehold rights.
B. assign the lessor's rights.
C. sublease the property.
D. not sublease the property.

8. Which of these lease arrangements is motivated by improving the tenant's immediate cash flow?

A. Percentage lease
B. Sale and leaseback
C. Fixed lease
D. Index lease

9. A lease in which the tenant pays a portion of the building's operating expenses is a

A. graduated lease.
B. percentage lease.
C. gross lease.
D. net lease.

10. A tenant who fails to vacate upon the expiration of an estate for years

A. is a holdover tenant.
B. must be evicted.
C. may automatically renew.
D. must give notice to extend.

11. Which lease would MOST LIKELY be of the longest duration?

A. Fixed lease
B. Index lease
C. Graduated lease
D. Ground lease

12. A temporary right of possession by a non owner of the property may be called any of these EXCEPT

A. tenancy.
B. leasehold.
C. estate.
D. freehold.

13. Which of the following is NOT a method of lease termination?

A. Expiration
B. Mutual cancellation
C. Negligence
D. Eviction

14. Which of these is required in a lease?

A. Option to renew
B. Recordation of the document
C. A formal legal description
D. Identification of the term and method to terminate

15. The only type of leasehold that would NOT be negotiated in advance with a landlord would be an

A. estate at sufferance.
B. estate from year to year.
C. estate for years.
D. estate at will.

16. Oral leases are

A. acceptable for terms of less than one year.
B. not enforceable in court.
C. not valid.
D. acceptable if the rental rate is less than $500.

17. William's lease is described as open-ended. This must be an estate

A. from year to year.
B. at will.
C. at sufferance.
D. for years.

18. An apartment tenant's right of quiet enjoyment means that

A. the landlord can never enter the property without the tenant's permission.
B. other tenants in the building must respect rules regarding noise.
C. the landlord must perform upkeep of the premises.
D. unless stated otherwise in the contract, the landlord must have the tenant's permission to enter the property with the exception of emergency situations.

19. The obligations of the landlord and tenant to each other are mostly dictated by

A. Michigan laws addressing rentals.
B. the Uniform Landlord and Tenant Act.
C. the terms of the lease contract.
D. common law.

20. The term of a lease

A. must be for a minimum period of one year.
B. may be altered by the landlord unilaterally.
C. may be reduced by a breach of contract.
D. will always require notice to terminate.

21. Who has a reversionary interest in leased property?

A. Lessor
B. Lessee
C. Possessor
D. Tenant

22. To legally remove a tenant from possession of the premises is called

A. mitigating damages.
B. actual eviction.
C. eviction.
D. holdover tenancy.

23. This lease exists for a fixed period of time and terminates automatically without notice by either party--an estate

A. at sufferance.
B. for years.
C. at will.
D. from year to year.

24. Which of the following acts by the landlord would be an act of negligence?

A. Failure to install window screens
B. Failure to replace air filters
C. Failure to replace a cracked window
D. Failure to repair a leaking gas heater

25. A contract that temporarily transfers the right to possession of a property is a/an

A. lease.
B. deed.
C. option.
D. tenancy.

Property Management

1. In Michigan, an agent who shows a The property manager's authority to represent the principal is established by

A. the express terms of the property management agreement.
B. the state and local Board of REALTORS® committee on property management.
C. local custom and tradition.
D. state laws on property management.

2. Property insurance that includes coverage for losses resulting from hail, explosion windstorm, aircraft, civil commotion, vehicles, and smoke from friendly fires is called

A. an insurance rider.
B. catastrophe insurance.
C. an endorsement clause.
D. extended coverage.

3. The property manager has budgeted for annual checks of the heating and air conditioning units and monthly replacement of air filters in all apartment units. This is an example of

A. capital replacement.
B. corrective maintenance.
C. preventative maintenance.
D. stabilized budgeting.

4. Several anchor tenants would most likely be found in a/an

A. strip shopping center.
B. regional shopping mall.
C. area without any other adjacent store.
D. neighborhood shopping center.

5. Which of the following functions would most likely be outside of a residential property manager's authority?

A. Dispatching repairmen
B. Checking credit histories, references, and employment status of potential tenants
C. Representing the owner in court proceedings such as evictions
D. Decisions regarding eviction of delinquent tenants

6. Which of these budgets will address the shortest period of time in the property management analysis?

A. Capital reserve budget
B. Stabilized budget
C. Management report
D. Operating budget

7. The first step in a property management relationship wherein the agent outlines the situation, needs, and benefits of professional management is called a/an

A. operating budget.
B. management proposal.
C. management agreement.
D. feasibility study.

8. All of the following have an insurable interest in real property EXCEPT a

A. tenant.
B. life tenant.
C. buyer.
D. seller.

9. Which of the following property management situations would be LEAST likely to have a resident manager?

A. A 350-unit apartment building
B. A mini-storage warehouse
C. A residential four-plex
D. A 300,000 square foot shopping center

10. Which of these retail properties is likely to be the smallest and most in need of close and easy access to a roadway and high visibility?

A. Strip shopping center
B. Anchor store
C. Neighborhood shopping center
D. Mall

11. Which property manager is LEAST likely to be compensated on a percentage of collections basis?

A. An apartment resident manager
B. A broker handling single-family rentals
C. A commercial property manager
D. A homeowner's association manager

12. A property manager's major function is

A. screening and locating tenants.
B. collecting rents.
C. preserving the value and quality of the owner's property.
D. residing on the property if the use is residential.

13. Which of these types of maintenance is the most difficult to predict and budget for?

A. Preventative maintenance
B. Reserve for capital replacement
C. Corrective maintenance
D. Construction

Taxation

1. Which of the following expenses may be deducted by a buyer when purchasing a new personal residence?

A. Appraisal fee
B. Discount points
C. Credit report cost
D. Mortgage insurance premium

2. According to the inheritance basis for computing gain, real property received by heirs will be taxed based on the

A. price the decedent paid.
B. market value on the date of the decedent's death minus any deferred taxes.
C. market value of the property on the date of the decedent's death.
D. price the decedent paid plus Improvements.

3. The Taxpayer Relief Act of 1997 provides which of the following?

A. A once-in-a-lifetime exclusion on capital gain for primary homeowners
B. Qualified first-time home buyers may withdraw up to $10,000 from a retirement fund without penalty to use toward the acquisition of a primary residence
C. Real estate practitioners to deduct their housing expenses
D. No penalty if an owner reinvests profit in 24 months

4. Closing expenses paid by the sellers are generally

A. not deductible.
B deductible against ordinary income.
C. added to the buyer's basis.
D. deductible against the selling price and profit.

5. An agent who wants to sell new cooperatives

A. must have held a license for no fewer than three years.
B. must be registered as a securities broker under Michigan's Uniform Securities Act.
C. must stay on-site until the building is completed.
D. may sell new cooperatives with only a real estate license

6. In order to claim the universal exclusion

A. the property must have been the principal residence for the last 24 months.
B. one of the spouses must be 55 on or before December 31 in the year the property is sold.
C. both of the spouses must be 55 on or before the date of closing.
D. the property must have been your primary residence for 2 of the last 5 years.

7. Which of the following is NOT deductible in home ownership?

A. Property taxes
B. Discount points
C. Mortgage interest
D. Principal

8. Jim and Stella Doen have sold their home for $122,000. They paid $68,500 in 1981 and added a pool for $12,000 in 1983 and a room addition for $7,500 in 1985. What is their adjusted basis?

A. $122,000
B. $ 80,500
C. $ 88,000
D. $ 68,500

9. The time frame to reinvest the sales proceeds from the sale of a rental property into a new rental is

A. 18 months after the first sale.
B. there is no rollover provision on rental property.
C. 24 months before or after the first sale.
D. 12 months after the first sale.

10. The time frame for reinvesting the sales proceeds from the sale of a personal residence into a new residence is

A. there is no rollover provision for personal residence.
B. 18 months after the first sale.
C. 12 months after the first sale.
D. 24 months before or after the first sale.

11. In the sale of a personal residence the taxpayer is taxed on

A. the net proceeds check.
B. the full sales price.
C. the full price less sales commission.
D. gain over $250,000 if she is single.

12. Fleishman sold his home for $149,000. He paid $72,000 in 1981 and added a pool for $14,500 in 1983 and a room addition for $7,200. What is his gain on the sale of this home?

A. $ 77,000
B. $149,000
C. $ 93,700
D. $ 55,300

13. Jim and Cathy Jenkins have sold their home for $121,000. They paid $69,000 in 1981 and in 1983 added a room for $12,000. If they buy a new home for $168,900, what is the adjusted basis of the new home?

A. $ 69,000
B. $121,000
C. $128,900
D. $ 81,000

Review Exam

1. Security deposits in a rental agreement legally belong to the

   A. landlord.
   B. tenant.
   C. state of Michigan.
   D. regulated financial institution.

2. Act 299, as amended, may be cited as the

   A. Code of Ethics.
   B. Occupational Code.
   C. Administrative Rules.
   D. Elliot-Larsen Civil Rights Act.

3. An action from a disciplinary hearing may include all of the following regarding a licensee EXCEPT

   A. censure.
   B. imprisonment for 1 year.
   C. revocation of license.
   D. a license limitation.

4. All on site expenses incurred by the Department to investigate out of state real estate promotions must be paid by the

   A. future buyers.
   B. Michigan general fund.
   C. Michigan broker involved in the promotion.
   D. Department.

5. As a licensed salesperson you can advertise using only your own name when

   A. renting another person's cottage for a fee.
   B. selling your own principal residence

   C. selling vacant property.
   D. exchanging properties for others for a fee.

6. The license of a real estate salesperson is delivered by the Department to the

   A. salesperson's employing broker.
   B. salesperson.
   C. Attorney General.
   D. Director of the Department.

7. A real estate salesperson, on receipt of a deposit from the buyer in a real estate transaction, must

   A. deposit the money in his or her personal account.
   B. deposit the money in his or her business account.
   C. deliver the money to the seller.
   D. deliver the money to his broker.

8. Under the Michigan Land Sales Act, a property report must be given to the purchaser

   A. before a contract is signed.
   B. immediately after a contract is signed.
   C. within 5 days after a contract.
   D. at the closing is signed.

9. When a principal associate broker ceases to be connected with a partnership or corporation, his or her license

   A. may be sold to another person, whether or not that person is associated with the firm.
   B. may be sold to another member of the firm.
   C. is automatically suspended.
   D. continues to be valid but may not be sold.

102

10. The license of each real estate salesperson shall be kept in the custody of the

A. Department.
B. broker who employs the salesperson.
C. salesperson.
D. broker and the salesperson.

11. The document received from each person or company prior to providing labor or materials to a construction project under the Michigan Construction Lien Act is known as the

A. Sworn Statement.
B. Notice of Commencement.
C. Notice of Furnishing.
D. Waiver of Lien.

12. MSHDA (Michigan State Housing Development Authority) permits all of the following EXCEPT

A. buyers may buy the home and rent it out for income.
B. buyers may finance used homes.
C. new homes must be constructed by a licensed builder.
D. buyers may finance used mobile homes.

13. Which of the following loans is covered by the Michigan Due on Sale Clause Act?

A. Real estate loans originated by federal savings banks
B. Federally chartered credit union loans
C. Mortgages without a due on sale clause
D. Real estate loans originated by state chartered lenders

14. Which of the following phrases between two broker is permitted under The Michigan Uniform State Antitrust Act?

A. "We shouldn't cooperate with any broker who cuts commission."
B. "Let's do something about his discount fee policy.'
C. "Everyone charges the same commission rate."
D. "Our company pays a 20% referral fee."

15. Which of the following is not permitted under Michigan's Wetland Protection Act in a designated wetland without a permit from the Department of Environmental Quality (DEQ)?

A. Fishing
B. Hunting
C. Dredging
D. Boating

16. Under Michigan's Mortgage Brokers, Lenders and Servicers Licensing Act, "any person, who directly or indirectly, makes or offers to make mortgage loans" is defined as a

A. broker.
B. lender.
C. servicer.
D. banker.

17. Private parties and other unregulated lenders may only charge individual borrowers a maximum rate of interest in Michigan of

    A. 11%.
    B. 15%.
    C. 7%.
    D. 25%.

18. Sam Snod is licensed as an individual broker in Michigan. He may advertise his listings under which of the following?

    A. Snod Realty, Co.
    B. Sam Snod Real Estate, Inc.
    C. Sam Snod
    D. Sam Snod, Broker

19. Which of the following selections MOST correctly identifies the person from which a licensed salesperson can directly receive a commission?

    A. The seller whose house the salesperson has listed.
    B. The buyer, providing the salesperson has established an agency relationship with the buyer.
    C. A broker licensed in any state.
    D. A broker under whom the salesperson is licensed.

20. A licensee who wants to renew their license in compliance with the renewal requirements must do all of the following EXCEPT

    A. return a new application for relicensure, with proper fee, to the Department.
    B. complete the approved continuing education courses.
    C. return the completed renewal form, with proper fee, to the Department.
    D. notify the Department of any change in name or address.

21. The Michigan Sellers Disclosure Act requires a seller to disclose which of the following to the buyer?

    A. The cost of improvements made by the seller.
    B. The loan amount the seller will be paying off.
    C. The price the seller paid for the property.
    D. The proximity of a farm in the area.

22. The maximum amount of time within which a broker is required to place earnest money deposits in his escrow account is two banking days

    A. from the date of receipt.
    B. following the signing of the offer by the offeror.
    C. from the date of the check.
    D. from the broker's knowledge that an offer to purchase is accepted by all parties.

23. Which of the following is correct according to the Michigan Security Deposits Act?

    A. A landlord is relieved of returning the unused portion of a security deposit to a tenant who fails to give the landlord his forwarding address within four days
    B. Security deposits may ultimately be used only to reimburse the landlord for cleaning purposes and repair damages to the premises
    C. A landlord who deposits a bond

with the Secretary of State may use the security deposit for any purpose he desires
    D. A landlord is relieved from giving the tenant inventory checklists if the premise is new construction being leased for the first time

24. A broker has just discharged a salesperson. The broker should do which of the following?

    A. Instruct the salesperson to complete all pending transactions within thirty days
    B. Surrender the salesperson's license to the Department within five days of the termination
    C. Remove the salesperson's license from the wall and keep it on file until all of the salesperson's transactions have been closed
    D. Give the salesperson his license to enable him to endorse the new broker's name and identification number on it

25. A licensee is required to carry his pocket card

    A. only when marketing residential properties.
    B. at all times during the period for which it is issued.
    C. when acting in the capacity indicated on the card.
    D. at all times while working unless the licensee is a broker.

26. Salesperson Sally Smith wishes to purchase a four-bedroom home from homeowner Mark Alot who currently has his home listed with Smiths' broker Tom Jones. Which of the following is true?

    A. Smith is required to make her intentions clearly known to Alot that she is the purchasing party
    B. Smith will be required to set the purchase up through a silent third party buyer purchasing on her behalf
    C. Smith may purchase the home as if she were not a licensed real estate agent
    D. Jones must purchase the property and then resell it to Smith

27. A landlord may place all BUT which of the following in residential leases according to the Michigan Truth in Renting Act?

    A. A provision which holds the landlord harmless for his negligence
    B. A provision which requires a landlord to mitigate damages incurred by a tenant breaking his lease prematurely
    C. Provisions which require the landlord to maintain the premises in reasonable repair
    D. A provision which establishes that the landlord does not discriminate

28. Under which of the following circumstances may a real estate salesperson lawfully refuse to show a property to a minority prospect who has specifically asked to see it?

    A. When the owner has exercised his exemption under Michigan Fair Housing Law and designated the property as not available to minority prospects
    B. When the real estate agent sincerely believes that such a showing will cause block busting
    C. When the owner is out of town and has instructed the real estate

salesperson that no showing may be made in his absence
D. When the salesperson's broker asks the salesperson to divert any minorities to specific neighborhoods to avoid panic selling

29. Under Michigan Fair Housing Law, all BUT which of the following persons falls within a protected classification?

    A. A woman who is denied access to a property due to her gender
    B. A woman who is told a rental unit is not available because she is an attorney
    C. A Catholic priest whose offer to purchase a home is denied due to the fact that he is not Jewish
    D. A family who is told no rental units are available to families with children

30. Who is responsible for paying the Michigan Transfer Tax when a deed is recorded?

    A. Buyer
    B. Seller
    C. Listing broker
    D. Selling broker

31. A person who engages the service of another, under contractual agreement for the purpose of affecting that person's legal relations with third persons is a/an

    A. principal.
    B. customer.
    C. agent.
    D. subagent.

32. A person who essentially holds the position of trustee in an agency relationship is called a/an

    A. ostensible agent.
    B. tort.
    C. fiduciary.
    D. client.

33. Which type of listing arrangement entitles the broker employed to a commission no matter who sells the property during the listing period?

    A. An open listing
    B. An exclusive right-to-sell listing
    C. A net listing
    D. An exclusive agency listing

34. A listing that allows the property owner to pay a commission only to the broker who is the efficient and procuring cause of the sale is a/an

    A. open listing.
    B. exclusive listing.
    C. net listing.
    D. multiple listing.

35. Ownership of personal property can be transferred at settlement by the use of a/an

    A. estoppel certificate.
    B. bill of sale.
    C. bailment.
    D. easement.

36. Broker Jones lists a property for a period of 60 days. During the term of the listing Broker Jones introduces Buyer Green to the property. Two weeks after the listing expires Buyer Green negotiates a sale directly with the seller. Under these circumstances, which of the following is true?

    A. Buyer Green would owe the broker a commission for introducing them to the property
    B. Buyer Green and the seller cannot, by law, negotiate directly
    C. Broker Jones has NO recourse against any party for his fee
    D. Broker Jones would be due a commission if he had a carryover clause in the listing contract

37. The seller of an apartment building agrees to pay a broker 6% of the first $100,000 of the sale price and 3½ % of the amount over $100,000. If the sale price is $119,900, what is the broker's commission?

    A. $7,140
    B. $6,697
    C. $4,197
    D. $4,694

38. If a broker is to receive a fee of 7% of the actual sale price of a house, how much less will he earn if the seller reduces the price of $63,000 by $5,000?

    A. $175
    B. $260
    C. $350
    D. $700

39. A broker's agency policy is that the company will not practice dual agency. This most often means the

    A. company will not represent the buyer and seller in the same transaction.
    B. company will not show the same property to more than one buyer.
    C. agents cannot show company listings to buyers.
    D. broker will not advocate the position of his agents.

40. Salespersons may accept compensation of their predetermined share of the commission from

    A. the multiple listing service.
    B. the owner of the property.
    C. their employing broker.
    D. a cooperating broker.

41. A broker's agency relationship with buyers and sellers can best be described as

    A. special agent.
    B. general agent.
    C. implied agent.
    D. ostensible agent.

42. The least protection for the GRANTEE is provided by

    A. general warranty deed.
    B. quit claim deed.
    C. trustee's deed.
    D. special warranty deed.

43. A condominium that is broken into 52 one-week time intervals and purchasers are able to buy as many intervals as they wish is known as

    A. limited common elements.
    B. time-sharing condominiums.
    C. incremental condominiums.
    D. leasehold condominiums.

44. A Warranty Deed provides the LEAST protection for which of the following

A. grantor.
B. mortgagor.
C. grantee.
D. mortgagee.

45. The process in which land is accumulated by the gradual washing or motion of water is known as

A. accretion.
B. avulsion.
C. reliction.
D. riparian.

46. The chronological record of all conveyances AND encumbrances affecting the record title to real property is known as

A. title insurance policy.
B. chain of title.
C. abstract.
D. title report.

47. All of the following are essential elements of a valid deed EXCEPT

A. the grantor's signature.
B. legally adequate description.
C. consideration.
D. the grantee's signature.

48. A title that is "indefeasible" is one that cannot be

A. recorded.
B. conveyed.
C. voided.
D. inherited.

49. If Mr. Thomas has a life estate interest and rents the property to Mr. Hearns, upon Mr. Thomas' death, Mr. Hearns' leasehold will

A. terminate.
B. not be affected.
C. be converted to a freehold.
D. automatically be renewed.

50. The process by which title to roads and other land is transferred BY a property owner TO the government is called

A. dedication.
B. demise.
C. forfeiture.
D. eminent domain.

51. The right of the government to ownership of property which is left by a deceased property owner who leaves no will and dies without descendants is

A. eminent domain.
B. inchoate.
C. testate.
D. escheat.

52. The "unity of Person" is present in which of the following forms of ownership?

A. Ownership in severalty
B. Joint tenancy
C. Tenancy in common
D. Tenancy by the entirety

53. Which of the following is the document that defines the operative rules for a condominium complex and its individual unit owners?

A. Master Deed
B. Proprietary Lease
C. Bylaws
D. Declaration

54. A quitclaim deed is frequently used to

A. remove a cloud on a title.
B. remove an escrow.
C. terminate a power of attorney.
D. evict a tenant.

55. If the grantor delivers a deed to the grantee in which the name of the grantee has been left out inadvertently, the deed is

A. invalid.
B. voidable.
C. valid.
D. forged.

56. The estate in real property with the least bundle of rights is

A. tenancy at will.
B. fee simple absolute.
C. fee simple subject to a condition subsequent.
D. tenancy at sufferance.

57. The type of estate that is the most freely inheritable and transferable is a/an

A. estate in remainder.
B. life estate.
C. fee simple estate.
D. estate in reversion.

58. An example of personal property is

A. household furnishings.
B. wall -to-wall carpeting.
C. built-in dishwasher.
D. garbage disposal.

59. A lessee renting under the terms of a net lease is least likely to pay for which of the following?

A. Property taxes
B. Insurance premiums for fire
C. Telephone service
D. Mortgage debt service

60. The death of a lessor usually affects the lease by which of the following?

A. It is rescinded
B. It is considered void
C. It is not affected
D. It is defeated

61. All real estate sales contracts must be in writing to avoid disputes over oral negotiations according to the

A. Real Estate Settlement Procedures Act.
B. Statute of Frauds.
C. Truth - in - Lending Act.
D. Parol Evidence Rule.

62. A land contract vendee's interest is considered to be which of the following?

A. Actual title
B. Non-freehold
C. Personal only
D. Equitable title

63. The Uniform Vendor and Purchaser Risk Act protects which party in the event the property is destroyed prior to the closing?

   A. The buyer
   B. The lender
   C. The seller
   D. The broker

64. Prospective buyer Suzie Sweet gives broker Lance Reins a $2,000 deposit with an offer to purchase one of his listings. The $2,000 may best be referred to as

   A. an assignment.
   B. mutual assent.
   C. earnest money.
   D. good consideration.

65. If a seller defaults on a purchase agreement, the buyer may be able to force him to perform by suing for

   A. rescission.
   B. specific performance.
   C. Statute of Frauds.
   D. damages.

66. To be valid, an option must be supported by

   A. good consideration.
   B. valuable consideration.
   C. legal tender.
   D. earnest money.

67. A contract signed by a minor is generally considered

   A. void.
   B. unenforceable.
   C. voidable.
   D. illegal.

68. A landlord leases a piece of property under an Estate for Years. The future interest of the landlord is best referred to as which of the following?

   A. Equitable interest
   B. Reversionary interest
   C. Compound interest
   D. Executed interest

69. The repayment of a financial obligation over a period of time in a series of periodic installments is known as

   A. amortization.
   B. appreciation.
   C. loan - to - value ratio.
   D. equitable conversion.

70. A mortgage used in the purchase of residential property which, in addition to real property, covers certain personal property items and equipment is known as a/an

   A. open mortgage.
   B. package mortgage.
   C. blanket mortgage.
   D. participation mortgage.

71. The money for Federal Housing Administration (FHA) and Veterans Administration (VA) loans is provided by

   A. FHA and VA only.
   B. private investors only.
   C. any qualified lending institution.
   D. the Internal Revenue Service.

72. The Federal Housing
    Administration (FHA)

    A. provides loan money.
    B. insures loan money.
    C. guarantees loan money.
    D. discounts loan money.

73. The Federal Truth-in-Lending Act
    covers all of the following EXCEPT

    A. assumption of a loan.
    B. annual percentage rate.
    C. finance charges.
    D. points.

74. A buyer finances a piece of property
    with a conventional mortgage. The
    lender is referred to as which of the
    following

    A. vendor.
    B. mortgagor.
    C. trustee.
    D. mortgagee.

75. A "certificate of eligibility" is
    issued under which of the
    following types of loans?

    A. VA
    B. FHA
    C. Graduated payment mortgage
    D. Renegotiable rate mortgage

76. A $20,000 loan is to be paid off at the
    rate of $7.50 per $1,000 per month. If
    the annual taxes of $360 and the 3-year
    insurance premium of $54 on the
    property are to be prorated and included,
    what will be the first total monthly
    payment?

    A. $107
    B. $178
    C. $182
    D. $234

77. During one year a man paid an
    average of $126 a month interest on
    his loan. If he was in the 28% tax
    bracket and all the interest for that
    year was deductible from taxable
    income, approximately how much
    credit could he apply from this
    deduction?

    A. $ 35
    B. $ 42
    C. $353
    D. $423

78. Carlos Murphy contracted to sell his
    house to Charlie Crab for $135,000.
    The sale was contingent on Crab's
    obtaining a $90,000 loan. Murphy
    agreed to pay four points. The
    amount that Murphy will pay when
    the loan is secured is

    A. $6,400.
    B. $1,350.
    C. $3,600.
    D. $ 900.

79. Pledging real property as collateral
    for a loan is

    A. trust deed.
    B. amortization.
    C. acceleration.
    D. hypothecation.

80. A vendee is one who

    A. sells or offers to sell.
    B. buys or offers to buy.
    C. loans money.
    D. borrows money.

81. Which of the following best describes a sale and leaseback transaction?

   A. The seller gets a return on the purchase in the form of rental
   B. The property is sold on condition that the new owner lease it back to the seller at the time title passé
   C. The buyer keeps capital in inventories, rather than in realty
   D. The rental that the seller pays is not income tax deductible

82. Truth-in-Lending laws apply to

   A. commercial loan transactions involving real property.
   B. residential real estate mortgages.
   C. all personal property transactions.
   D. unconscionable contracts.

83. An "acceleration clause" found in a promissory note or mortgage would mean that

   A. upon the happening of a certain.
   B. event the entire amount of the unpaid.
   C. balance becomes due.

   D. payments may not be made more frequently than specified.

84. A "suit to quiet title" refers to

   A. court action to remove a cloud on a title.
   B. legal action to prevent noise pollution.

   C. court order for the performance of a contract.
   D. statutory claim to the right of dower.

85. The loss in value of a property due to wear and tear of the structure is

   A. functional obsolescence.
   B. physical deterioration.
   C. economic obsolescence.
   D. subrogation.

86. A pre-existing use of land which does not conform to the zoning ordinance but which may legally remain is

   A. spot - zoning.
   B. non-conforming use.
   C. reversion.
   D. a variance.

87. In government zoning, the distance from the front of a building to the street is a/an

   A. cul-de-sac.
   B. egress.
   C. setback.
   D. ingress.

88. A half mile square is equal to

   A. 320 acres.
   B. 160 acres.
   C. 80 acres.
   D. 40 acres.

89. Which of the following liens normally takes priority over the others?

   A. Judgment liens
   B. Mortgage liens
   C. Mechanics' liens
   D. Real estate tax liens

90. Which of the following might be classified as functional obsolescence?

A. Exterior needs painting
B. Property fronts on a busy Expressway
C. Property has a one - car garage
D. Neighborhood is 50 years old

91. Real estate values are most affected by

A. location.
B. availability.
C. appraisal.
D. national trends.

92. Zoning is done by authority of

A. elected officials.
B. law of eminent domain.
C. police power.
D. petition.

93. The right of eminent domain refers to

A. the right of every American citizen to own property.
B. an organization's right to condemn property pending an improvement that is for the good of the community.
C. an institution or individual acquiring land by grant from the government.
D. the government's right to acquire or authorize others to acquire title to property for public use.

94. One owner wishes to develop a 10-unit apartment building on his property in an area zoned for single family residences. What type of legal process should be requested?

A. Nonconforming use
B. Subrogation
C. Building permit
D. Variance

95. Regulations established by the government setting forth the construction requirements of structures are best described by which term?

A. Conveyance
B. Devise
C. Common law
D. Building code

96. Mr. Doe requests that his single family, residential property be rezoned to multiple family so that he can construct an additional house on his lot, rent it out and make additional income. The neighborhood Mr. Doe lives in is all zoned single family residential. If the city grants his request, it would best be described as which of the following?

A. Exclusionary zoning
B. Spot zoning
C. Cumulative zoning
D. Cluster zoning

97. A recorded notice of a current lawsuit involving title to real property is a/an

A. lis pendens.
B. writ of execution.
C. attachment.
D. order to show cause.

98. Which of the following encumbrances would constitute a lien on real property?

A. Easement
B. Encroachment
C. Restriction
D. Mortgage

99. A chanting religious group bought a house in a subdivision and organized it into a commune. A broker, eager to make some quick profits, began to canvass this neighborhood, soliciting listings by inquiring whether the owners knew who had just moved into the area and leaving the firm's business card. Which term best describes the broker's marketing program?

A. Redlining
B. Lawful solicitation
C. Block busting
D. Steering

100. The Civil Rights Act of 1866 prohibits discrimination in housing on the basis of

A. mental or physical disability.
B. race.
C. sex.
D. familial status.

114

Introduction to Real Estate Principles

1. D.   The greater the supply of any commodity in comparison to demand, the lower the value will be. It does not necessary follow, however, that a large supply of a product will lead to more or less demand. For example, if manufacturers of a popular soft drink flood the market with that product, demand for the product will remain relatively stable even though the market has been saturated.

2. B.   A free market concept provides sufficient time for informed buyers and sellers to effect a mutually beneficial transaction without undue or external influences. The market is open to all buyers with sufficient funds to purchase and all sellers who make their property available for sale.

3. B.   Location of a parcel of land has the greatest effect on its value because the characteristic of immobility makes the land unique and permanent.

4. D.   Improvements that are not attached to the land are considered personal property.

5. B.   Highest and best use is achieved when land is improved through the use of capital, labor, and management.

6. A.   The National Association of REALTORS® is the trade association of the real estate industry whose members are known as REALTORS®. To be a REALTOR® a person must be licensed by an individual state and must be a member of a local board or association.

7. B.   The listing agreement is a written contract between the property owner and a real estate firm.

8. B.   All physical and economic characteristics are considered in determining the highest and best use of land.

9. D.   Immobility, meaning that land cannot be moved or relocated, is a major factor affecting land value. This physical characteristic of land is the primary distinction between real property and tangible personal property.

10. C.   The number of real estate agents in the marketplace has little or no effect upon supply and demand in the market.

11. D.   These are examples of government or public land use controls.

115

12. C.   Real estate licensees are not limited to selling properties. Other career areas in the real estate profession include appraising, financing, building and developing, property management, and consulting.

13. D.   Streets, highways, and parks belong to the public and are governed by city, state and federal regulations.

14. B.   Successful real estate licensees do not use techniques such as the "hard sell" but rather work diligently at assisting buyers, sellers, lessors and lessees in all transactions in which they are involved.

15. A.   Heterogeneity, meaning that each piece of property is unique, is a physical characteristic of real estate.

16. D.   Heterogeneity, meaning that each piece of property is unique, is a physical characteristic of real estate.

17. C.   Individual private ownership of land is the allodial system of ownership. Because the general public has a vested interest in the use of all land, however, the individual owner's use of the land is governed by land use controls and restrictions.

18. A.   An investor must consider the highest and best use of the land, not the highest and best use of improvements.

19. D.   The completion occurs at settlement, also known as closing, which is the act of adjusting and prorating credits, charges, and settlement costs to conclude the transaction.

20. B.   Because financing is so important, real estate salespersons should have a day-to-day working knowledge of the rates, terms and conditions of various loan programs.

21. D.   Personal property is everything that is not the land or items which are permanently attached to the land.

22. D.   Investment is the outlay of money with the intention of deriving income or profit which exceeds the initial outlay.

23. A.   An increase in the utilization of land creates more uses of the land and therefore increases the potential for income generation.

24. B.   Liquidity is not usually an objective in real estate investment. Real estate is a non-liquid investment. Once purchased, real estate investments typically cannot be sold quickly without a loss.

25. D. Personal property is everything that is not real property, that which is not attached to land.

Property Ownership and Interests

1. D Michigan law does not recognize a husband's right to property owned by his wife alone.

2. C A life estate is a freehold estate that provides ownership, possession, and control for the life of the named individual(s) as in this case.

3. B The essential difference between the two forms of estate is the period of time for which each is given. A life estate has an indeterminable period of ownership, the life of the owner, making it a freehold estate. An estate for years has a limited, quantifiable, fixed period making it a leasehold estate.

4. B Two ways that ownership of a cooperative differs from condominium ownership are (1) a co-op owner has shares of stock in a corporation evidenced by a proprietary lease, and (2) the cooperative common areas are owned by a corporation in fee.

5. D An emblement is something growing that requires planting each season with the intent to harvest. As such, it is defined in law as personal property. Examples include crops such as corn, wheat, and tomatoes.

6. D Condominium property is not wholly mortgaged, although individual units may be. In order to create a condominium, a Declaration (or master deed), Articles of Association, and bylaws must be recorded.

7. A Dower is an automatic life estate owned by a wife in inheritable property which is owned by the husband alone.

8. A The term "right of survivorship" refers to the right of the surviving co-owners to automatically receive the interest of the deceased co-owner upon his or her death.

9. B An estate that automatically renews itself for another period at the end of each term unless one party gives notice of termination to the other is a periodic estate or estate from year to year.

10. A The wife must sign the deed to release her dower at the time of sale.

11. A The real estate term for an improvement both on and to the land is fixture. At one time, the object was personal property or chattel, but once it becomes part of the real estate by attachment, it is no longer personal property.

12. A   This is the most complete form of ownership.

13. C   Upon the death of the landlord, the estate for years is still binding on the heirs.

14. C   Personal property is everything that is not real property. Another term for personal property is chattel. Chattel is everything that is readily movable, such as furniture, cars, and jewelry.

15. D   The dormant mineral rights must be re-recorded if owned by someone other than the property owner or the rights revert to the actual title holder of the property.

16. A   The person receiving the title upon the death of the life tenant is called the remainderman. Jennifer's estate is an estate in remainder.

17. A   Joint tenancy is evidenced by the co-owners having equal percentages of ownership, receiving title at the same time from the same source, having the right to undivided possession of the property and the right of survivorship.

18. C   An estate for years conveys an interest for a fixed period of any length.

19. C   Real estate includes all naturally growing things such as trees, shrubbery and plants.

20. D   Fee simple absolute contains the largest bundle of ownership rights possible.

21. B   Chattel, another name for personal property, is conveyed by a document called a bill of sale.

22. D   Tenancy at sufferance is not a form of concurrent ownership, but instead describes tenants who retain possession without the permission of the landlord.

23. D   Periodic estates and estates for years are examples of leasehold estates. They are both estates of limited duration. An estate for years exists for a fixed period of time only, whereas a periodic estate automatically renews itself for another period at the end of each term unless notice is given.

24. D   No buildings are set forth (or required to be set forth) in the site condominium development.

25. B   Tenancy in common is ownership held by co-owners which gives each owner an interest which is inheritable.

26. B   Qualified fee contains a defeasance clause so that ownership lasts only as long as the receiver uses it for the purpose specified by the grantor.

27. C   Before a timeshare can be offered for sale, its ownership must be structured as a condominium, not as a cooperative. The purchasers of the timeshare are receiving ownership for a stated period of time.

28. D   Once a new construction condominium purchase agreement is signed; it is not binding until nine business days after the developer delivers the prescribed condominium documents to the purchaser.

29   B   The leasehold estate, in the form of a proprietary lease, provides the right to possession of an apartment and use of the common areas.

30. B   The Uniform Commercial Code allows the mortgagee to hold a security interest in personal property when the purchase includes personal property such as equipment, inventory or trade fixtures.

31. B   "Definite termination date" is the benchmark for defining an estate for years.

32. C   Tenancy in common is an estate characterized by two or more owners who hold title to property at the same time with no rights of survivorship, whereas joint tenancy and tenancy by entireties provide for the right of survivorship. Another characteristic of tenancy in common is differing percentages of ownership between Virginia and Bill, which is not possible in join tenancy or tenancy by entireties interest. Virginia and Bill do not have an estate for years, which is the relationship between landlords and tenants.

33. B   Trade fixtures are items of personal property that a business operator installs.

34. B   Estate defines a person's rights or interest in real property.

35. B   A fee simple estate with a condition or limitation attached is termed a defeasible estate, often used when someone wishes to donate land to a church or school for a specific purpose.

36. C   Sam is a tenant at sufferance during eviction. At one time Sam had legal right to possession, but he no longer has the permission of the landlord to continue to possess the property.

37. C   A proprietary lease is the document that evidences occupancy in a cooperative.

38. C   Upon a divorce, an estate by the entireties automatically becomes tenancy in common, in which the right of survivorship is eliminated. The parties, however, can create a joint tenancy if they wish.

39. A   When title is held in the name of only one person or entity; it is ownership in severalty.

40. C The declaration or master deed to a condominium may contain all of the following: The legal description of the condominium facility, the height, width, and length of each unit; and a right to first refusal clause, which allows the association the first opportunity to purchase a unit if the owner wishes to sell. It would not contain owner's names, which would be found on future individual deeds.

41. C Property taxes and mortgage interest on a condominium are tax-deductible if it is your primary residence.

42. B The law that governs the financing of personal property is called the Uniform Commercial Code or the UCC. The UCC provides for the lender to retain a security interest in the personal property until the lender is paid in full.

43. B Of the four forms of ownership stated, the only one that has all four unities is joint tenancy.

44. D Fee simple does not have to be conveyed as an estate in severalty. It can be conveyed to joint owners, common tenants, or tenants by the entirety.

45. C Freehold estates are ownership estates for an undetermined length of time, such as fee simple and life estates.

Michigan Real Estate License Laws and Rules

1. B The department does NOT have the authority to dictate a prison term for violators, which is instead up to the court in which the case is prosecuted.

2. C This time frame is mandated by the Occupational Code.

3. B The Occupational Code requires a broker or associate broker to sign all escrow checks. There can be a co-signatory authorized by the broker that is not a broker or associate broker.

4. D Earl acted in the capacity of an agent by engaging in more than 6 sales in a 12 month period, therefore he could be found in violation of license law. He will not receive any credit toward his broker license because of this violation of the law.

5. D Selling your own listing with full agency disclosure is good business practice and not a violation of license law.

6. A The only property a salesperson may sell "by owner" is his or her principal residence. All other licensee-owned properties must be sold through a licensed real estate broker.

7. A   Failure to disclose to a purchaser or lessee of real property that a former occupant has or is suspected of having a disability is an activity for which a licensee will NOT be subject to disciplinary action.

8. B   A broker is allowed to pay a licensee commission or other income the licensee earned while licensed to that broker after the licensee leaves the broker's employ whether the individual is licensed with another broker or unlicensed at the time.

9. A   An individual who operates under a duly executed power of attorney is known as an attorney-in-fact.

10. D   Property promoted in Michigan must be handled by a licensed Michigan broker in accordance with the Michigan out of State Land Sales Act.

11. A   Michigan law states that you must be licensed in accordance with the Appraiser's law in order to appraise or offer to appraise real estate.

12. C   The Occupational Code requires money to be deposited within two banking days of the broker's knowledge of an accepted offer.

13. A   Salespersons are prohibited from accepting a commission or any other valuable consideration from anyone other than their employing broker.

14. C   Pocket cards are signed only by the new broker. Salespersons are not required to sign their pocket card when transferring.

15. D   An attorney-in-fact has the power of attorney to represent another and to make decisions for that person.

16. D   All salespersons and brokers, whether working full or part time, must be licensed.

17. C   Brokers must display all licenses issued to them in a conspicuous position in their place of business.

18. B   The agent must present the second offer if there is NO clause in the listing agreement stating that once an offer has been accepted, the broker shall stop marketing the property.

19. D   Examination scores are valid for one year from the date the exam was taken and passed. If the application has not been made within that time, the examination must be retaken.

20. B   Michigan license law and rules dictate that an associate broker's or salesperson's license will be issued only to individuals. Further, a licensee must operate his or her business in the name under which the license is issued.

21. C   Brokers who do not cooperate with each other are not in violation of license law or rule unless they represented to the seller that they would cooperate.

22. C   An authorized representative of the department has the authority to enter a broker's place of business during normal business hours and ask for and receive any and all documents pertaining to an investigation from any licensee in that office.

23. D   The department requires all license applicants to pass a written examination. If an applicant has a verifiable physical disability, the department will provide an exam that meets the applicant's needs.

24. A   Salespersons are only allowed to accept compensation in a real estate transaction from their employing broker.

25. A   If the department revoked a broker's license, the licenses of all licensees in the office will be automatically suspended pending a change of employer and the issuance of a new license.

26. D   A licensee may not accept or charge a commission, fee, or valuable consideration from a seller when the license is the purchaser without the seller's prior written consent to the specified commission.

27. C   Being licensed by the state does not necessitate MLS membership. After being licensed and working with a broker who is a REALTOR®, MLS membership is possible.

28. A   An Associate Broker satisfies the same licensing requirements as a Broker.

29. D   Michigan license law states that a nonresident must meet the Michigan requirements for licensure and sign an irrevocable consent to service of process to conduct business in Michigan. He or she does not have to be a resident of this state.

30. D   Salespersons cannot close a real estate transaction or alter any of the figures except under the direct supervision of their broker.

31. B   This definition describes a broker.

32. C   Michigan license law requires broker candidates to prove 90 clock hours of classroom study and 3 years full time in the field of real estate or in a field

determined by the department to be relevant and related. The department will not issue a license to anyone under the age of 18.

33. B   A salesperson can perform acts a broker is authorized to perform while under a broker's supervision but may not form or operate a real estate business without the supervision of a broker.

34. C   License law further states that if the analysis is in writing, it must state in boldface type: **THIS IS A MARKET ANALYSIS, NOT AN APPRAISAL, AND WAS PREPARED BY A LICENSED REAL ESTATE BROKER OR ASSOCIATE BROKER, NOT A LICENSED APPRAISER.**

35. B   A license can be suspended or revoked when a licensee makes any substantial and willful misrepresentation. To make an intentional false statement to induce someone to contract is a violation of license law.

36. C   No licensee may act in the real estate practice without first receiving his or her license and pocket card. The licensee must carry the card at all times when conducting real estate business.

37. C   In a limited partnership, the general partner must be an associate broker for the partnership to receive a broker's license.

38. D   Licensees must be able to prove that they disclosed to the seller, in writing, that they are a licensee prior to purchasing a property. Further, when selling property they own, licensees must inform a purchasers, in writing, that they are the owner whether they own the property directly or indirectly.

39. B   State license law does NOT require the licensee to join the local association of REALTORS®. Joining the local, state, or national association is voluntary and not state mandated.

40. D   A false statement regarding an important matter in a real estate transaction to induce someone to enter into a contract is called misrepresentation.

41. A   Every listing must be completely filled out prior to the seller signing it. The seller must receive a true copy at the time of signing. All listings must have a definite expiration date.

42. A   The state's police power is designed to protect the health, safety, welfare, and property of its citizens. Licensure protects the public against fraudulent or unscrupulous acts by agents.

43. A   Giving unauthorized legal counsel is prohibited by law. A real estate broker or salesperson may not prepare documents or give a legal opinion on the validity of any legal document.

44. B   Membership in the National Association of REALTORS® is strictly voluntary but is available for those who are licensed to transact real estate in Michigan.

Agency

1. C   In most cases the agency relationship established between a broker and the principal is a special agency.

2. D   Conduct can create a binding contract upon either the agent or the principal or both.

3. B   A subagent is someone who the principal authorizes their agent to enlist in accomplishing the purpose of the agency agreement. Therefore, the selling broker is a subagent unless he is representing the buyer.

4. B   Both contracts and conduct can create an agency relationship.

5. A   Due to the previous contract with the buyer, the agent has an absolute duty of confidentiality that lasts forever.

6. C   Michigan requires that written agency disclosure be provided prior to the disclosure of any confidential information by the buyer or the seller.

7. C   A multiple listing service is a network of brokerages.

8. D   An express agency would have been openly stated and agreed to whether in writing or orally.

9. D   The brokerage firm does not practice designated agency and is the agent of the buyer and seller, not the individual salespersons. Therefore, a dual agency is in effect.

10. D   By omitting material facts, Jordan misrepresented the home. He should have disclosed the room addition to the buyers regardless of the seller's instructions even though he tested all of the plugs. Jordan is not an electrician or inspector.

11. D   This is referred to as a multiple listing service, which allows more extensive marketing of member firms' properties through more offices.

12. D   After having been agreed upon by broker and client, commission is stipulated in the agency contract.

13. D   Michigan law requires that all third-party money must be deposited in the broker's escrow account within two banking days of the broker's knowledge of the seller's acceptance of an offer. Therefore, it is in the agent's best interest to turn the check over to his broker to assure that when the offer is accepted the money will be deposited in accordance with the law.

14. D   Agency disclosure forms are required prior to the disclosure of any confidential information to make it clear to all of the involved parties wherein loyalties and representation lie.

15. B   The broker was lied to when he made his inquiry and did not intend to deceive the buyer with this lack of disclosure; therefore, this is an example of innocent misrepresentation.

16. A   The buyer or seller may be the party responsible for paying the commission, depending upon the agreement of all parties involved.

17. A   The Michigan Anti-Trust Act is enforced by the courts and not the Department. If an action is taken regarding violation of license law, the Department may impose any of the penalties prescribed in Article 6 of the Occupational Code.

18. C   The party responsible for payment of the commission when a buyer's broker is involved is negotiated within the transaction.

19. B   Agency relationships are between the brokerage and the public; the broker is in a dual agency situation and all parties must be informed in writing to keep the broker in compliance with Michigan law.

20. A   Michigan's agency disclosure law mandates that an agent must explain all agency relationships available under Michigan law prior to the disclosure of any confidential information.

21. D   Michigan law requires licensees to advise potential sellers and their agents of their agency relationship prior to the disclosure of any confidential information.

22. A   Although separate salespeople are representing the buyer and the seller, the brokerage for which both salespeople work is representing both buyer and seller, thus creating a dual agency.

23. A   A buyer's broker as described above would be a special agent, establishing no authority for the broker to sign an offer or counteroffer.

24. B   If disclosure was delivered by certified mail the buyer would have 120 hours to terminate the contract in writing. If the disclosure is delivered in person, the buyer has 72 hours.

25. C   Estoppel is a means of establishing an agency relationship but not a means of terminating it.

26. A   An agent licensed in Michigan must make the Seller's Disclosure Form available at his or her place of business.

27. A   A special agency gives no power to the agent to bind the principal to a contract.

28. C   The duty of disclosure is owed to both parties. The duties of skill, care, and loyalty are owed only to the agent's principal.

29. A   Agency by estoppel occurs if an individual claims incorrectly that someone is his or her agent, and a third party relies on this information. Armstrong made this representation to a third party, and can not retract that representation; thus a valid agency relationship exists.

30. B   This action would be a violation of antitrust law because competing brokers who form an agreement to set commission rates are guilty of price fixing.

31. B   An act of omitting an important fact is misrepresentation, even when one fails to ask.

32. A   The principal must not hinder the agent's efforts in providing the services agreed to in the agency agreement.

33. A   Commingling of funds is the unlawful handling of other people's money and violates the broker's duty of accounting as set forth by Michigan license and agency law.

34. B   The client is the principal to whom the agent owes fiduciary duty.

35. D   A salesperson must conduct all business under direction of the broker. The broker has ultimate control over all business operations, including advertisements. The listings are the property of the broker and not the agent. The broker operates all trust accounts.

36. A   Conflicts of interest and dissatisfaction by one or both parties are very likely in a net listing.

37. A   Listing agreements typically create special agency, granting the agent no power to enter a contract as in the case of universal or general agency. This listing is expressed (that is, in writing) and not implied.

38. B   The listing agreement establishing an agency relationship between the broker and the seller has historically been the most common agency relationship.

39. D   A broker is entitled to her commissions if she produces a buyer who is ready, willing, and able to complete the terms of the transaction.

40. C   Contracts (expressed) and conduct (implied) may be separately or jointly responsible for establishing an agency relationship.

41. A   This is the definition of brokerage.

42. B   An MLS can increase the exposure of listed properties in the marketplace by offering them through many brokerages simultaneously.

43. A   Estoppel is a way in which agency may be created; it is not one of the duties of an agent.

44. A   This material fact should be disclosed to the buyer. An agent's primary duty is fair dealing to all parties, and only within the scope of fair dealing does the agent owe obedience, loyalty, and care.

Fair Housing

1. C   Familial status became a protected class under the Fair Housing Amendments of 1988 and so was not covered by the 1968 Fair Housing Act.

2. B   The Civil Rights Act of 1968 added religion as a protected class in addition to national origin and color.

3. A   All complaints are heard first at the state level by the state's enforcement agency. If unresolved within a specific period of time, they are then referred to a federal court.

4. A   Enforcement of the Fair Housing Act through HUD does not include the revocation of a real estate license. Revocation is a state remedy for a civil rights violation not a HUD remedy.

5. D   This law prohibits discrimination by any public or commercial facility or public transportation against persons with a mental or physical impairment that substantially limits one or more of their major life activities.

6. D   Landlords can use the phrase "adults only" to advertise elderly housing if all units are occupied by individuals age 62 or older. If 80 percent of the units have persons age 55 or older (under federal law), "adults only" advertising would also be permissible.

7. B   If a seller requests that a real estate salesperson not show the seller's property to minorities, the salesperson should withdraw from the listing relationship. No other broker will be able to assist in this illegal instruction.

8. A   An amendment to the 1968 Fair Housing Act requires all real estate brokerage offices to prominently display (not just anywhere) the Fair Housing poster. Failure to display the poster COULD imply failure to comply with federal law.

9. B   State civil rights laws can add protected classes to those specified by the federal law. However, state civil rights laws cannot increase the exemptions found under federal law.

10. A   The 1988 amendments to the federal Fair Housing Act prohibit discrimination based on familial status.

11. D   There is no provision in the 1988 amendments requiring mediation.

12. B   The Fair Housing Initiative Program provides funding for civil rights testers.

13. C   Sex was not a protected class under the 1968 Fair Housing Act, but gained protected status under the 1974 Housing and Community Development Act.

14. A   The landlord cannot deny a person with disabilities the right to make reasonable modifications to the premises to fit his or her life functions at the tenant's expense. A landlord is permitted to make adjustments and may bear the expenses, but is not required to do so.

15. C   Steering falls under the general prohibition of refusing to sell, rent, or negotiate the sale or rental of housing as a result of discriminatory practices.

16. C   Showing buyers properties based on affordability is permissible.

17. D   Refusing to make loans for a home purchase in a certain geographical area by discriminating on the basis of race, color, religion, sex, national origin, disability, or familial status is referred to as redlining.

18. D   The Civil Rights Act of 1866 was not designed to implement the Fair Housing Act because the Fair Housing Act was enacted 102 years after the Civil Rights Act of 1866.

19. A   The 1988 amendments to the Fair Housing Act of 1968 added familial status and persons with disabilities as protected classes.

20. C   It is legal to discriminate against smokers, but it is not legal to discriminate on the basis of race, sex, and familial status.

21. D   There is no provision in fair housing law that requires discrimination classes for license renewal.

22. C   This is the definition of a disability.

23. C   This exemption applies as long as the religious organization does not discriminate regarding who can be a member.

24. B   A real estate salesperson cannot base property selection on a buyer's sex (gender).

25. D   Pets are not a protected class; therefore, this statement does not indicate illegal behavior.

26. D   This law is far from being obsolete; in fact it provides the legal basis for all the other answer selections and has had a major impact on housing privileges.

27. A   The ADA is enforceable by all of the listed actions except a jail sentence.

28. C   The statute of limitations under the Elliot-Larsen Civil Rights Act is 180 days.

29. C   HUD has determined that the use of certain words in advertisements could have a discriminatory effect and this would trigger an investigation of the company's practices.

30. A   Warning a seller to place her home up for sale because minorities are moving into the area is an example of blockbusting.

31. A   At the end of the tenancy, the tenant must return the premises to their original condition at his own expense. The only exception is doorways. They do not have to be restored to their original condition.

32. B.   This broker would likely be accused of blockbusting, the practice of inducing owners to sell their property because of entry into the neighborhood of people who differ from current residents in race, national origin, religion, or other factors.

33. C   The Civil Rights Law of 1866 prohibits discrimination based on race without exception and under all circumstances. This law is also part of subsequent laws and supersedes any exemptions written into other fair housing laws.

Contract Law

1. **C**   This statement is true of an unenforceable contract. An unenforceable contract is not yet a void contract, and it may or may not involve a legal minor. It has not been fully performed.

2. **A**   Under these circumstances revocation results in termination.

3. **C**   The listing broker's identification has no relevance in the market value of the property.

4. **B**   This agreement is now voidable by either party because the termite damages exceed the agreed-upon amount for repairs. The contract is not void until the buyer and/or the seller decide to terminate their relationship. At this point, either party may agree to pay the excess amount. This contract would not be described as executed, since it is not fully performed, nor would it be described as unenforceable. Until the parties agree that the contract is void, it is still enforceable.

5. **C**   Accord and satisfaction is a new agreement between parties, often the result of a negotiated compromise.

6. **D**   The exclusive-right-to-sell listing obligates the seller to compensate the broker no matter who affects a sale of the property during the term of the listing, including the seller.

7. **A**   According to the Statute of Frauds, contracts involving the creation of interest or the conveyance of real property interest must be written to be enforceable in a court of law.

8. **D**   An exclusive agency listing selects only one broker as the agent with the owner reserving the right to sell the property himself without obligation to the broker.

9. **D**   Assignment is the transfer or sale of the contract rights the new owner acquired from the former owner.

10. **C**   An option is a right to purchase a given property by a specified date at a specified price.

11. **A**   Oral testimony alone is not sufficient to enforce a contract for the transfer of real estate.

12. **D**   Because only one promise is made, the option contract is unilateral.

13. D   Novation, which is the substitution of a new contract for a prior contract, is not a remedy for breach of contract.

14. D   An option contract requires the optionor (owner of the property) to comply with the agreement, but does not require the optionee (the nephew) to perform.

15. B   Value of comparable sales, a method appropriate for estimating the value for marketing purposes, is not an element of a contract.

16. B   A contract in which two parties make promises or performs acts is referred to as a bilateral contract.

17. A   Specific performance is a court decision which orders that the contract will be completed as originally agreed.

18. A   All legal contracts need not be executed, by agreement of the parties involved.

19. B   A land contract can be used for the sale of any type of property.

20. B   A broker producing a ready, willing, and able buyer or presenting an offer that meets the terms and conditions of the listing contract acceptable to the seller satisfies the tests entitling the broker to compensation. Either of these tests is sufficient.

21. A   The term "meeting of the minds" is synonymous with offer and acceptance.

22. D   Liquidated damages are those that are stipulated and agreed upon in the contract. In real estate, the most typical example of liquidated damages is forfeiture of earnest money should the buyer be unwilling or unable to execute the sales contract.

23. D   A fiduciary or agency relationship occurs upon signing of a listing contract. This contract states the employment terms for the broker, who will act as agent for the principal during the marketing of a property for lease, rent, sale, purchase, or exchange.

24. A   The court will only consider a contract that has all the essential elements. Therefore, the validity of the contract must first be determined.

25. D   The date is not an essential element of a contract.

26. D   Brokers rarely guarantee the sale of a property. That is, brokers do not typically promise that they will find buyers for the property or that there will be a closing. Instead, brokers promise that they will concentrate the efforts of their organization to find a buyer.

27. C   Such a contract is voidable by the party lacking full legal capacity.

28. C   An offer to purchase may not be terminated by buyer remorse after the offer has been accepted.

29. B   A broker employed under an exclusive-right-to-sell listing is entitled to the commission no matter who has procured or caused the sale.

30. D   A contract entered into under fraud (an intentional misrepresentation) is voidable by the person who relied on the misrepresentation and then entered into the contract.

31. D   An assignment of a contract transfers only the rights of the contract and does not eliminate the contractual obligations.

32. C   The "time is of the essence" clause is interpreted to mean that each deadline must be met as it occurs.

33. C   In an exclusive agency listing, the property is listed with only one broker, who acts as the sole agent. If the broker affects the sale, she earns the commission. However, if the seller affects the sale, no commission is paid.

34. A   A contract in which all conditions and terms have not been met, has not been completed or terminated.

35. C   Mutual mistake of a material fact by both parties causes the contract to be voidable but not void.

36. C   Undue influence is any improper or wrongful control or influence by one party to a contract over another.

37. B   Arm's length is the relationship between buyer and seller, both dealing from equal bargaining positions.

38. C   Violation of the legal capacity of the parties creates a voidable contract. A minor may hold an adult to a contract, whereas the adult cannot hold the minor responsible for his actions in the contract.

39. B   This statement describes an open listing, which allows the owner to list with several brokers and to compensate the broker who produces the ready, willing, and able buyer who is accepted by the seller.

40. C   The buyer's willingness to negotiate is not a test to determine commission entitlement, whereas the buyer's being ready, willing, and able to make the purchase is.

41. C   Earnest money is not used to buy down the interest rate of the mortgage loan. "Points" may be paid for this purpose.

42. D   The substitution of a new contract for a prior contract is a form of contract termination referred to as a novation. Novation typically involves the substitution of one party for another in the contract.

43. C   A materialman is a person providing material to a construction site and is not directly affected by the recording of a land contract.

44. A   An express contract is full agreement by all parties involved.

45. B   When the terms of a listing contract are changed by agreement of the parties, such as by extending the expiration date prior to expiration, it does not terminate the contract.

46. B   The principals do not form an agency relationship with each other.

47. B   A valid contract legally obligates all parties to abide by the terms and conditions of the contract.

48. C   The prime responsibility of the broker is to use his "best effort" to produce a ready, willing, and able purchaser or a purchaser acceptable to the seller.

49. A   A contract is an agreement between competent legal parties to do some legal act or to refrain from doing some legal act in exchange for consideration.

50. C   No two properties are exactly alike, but properties similar to the subject property in location, quality, and utility should be considered.

Transfers of Title

1. A   The quitclaim deed gives the least protection to the grantee and, therefore, the least liability to the grantor.

2. B   The judicial determination of a will's validity is referred to as a probate.

3. B   Because the executor of an estate is named in the will, the testator (that is, the person who drafts the will) names him.

4. D   The grantor is the one conveying the title.

5. A   This recording would provide constructive notice of the transfer, by which the world is bound by the knowledge that title is transferring.

6. A   Title examination usually begins with the present public record and works backward in time.

7. C   Harriman would sign a special warranty deed, which limits her liability to claims that may have occurred during the time that she held title.

8. D   There are 640 acres in the full section, divided by ¼ divided by ¼ divided by ½ = 20 acres.

9. D   Acknowledgement verifies the intent of the grantor and makes the deed eligible recording.

10. B   The greatest protection for the buyer is given in a General Warranty deed.

11. D   If a metes and bounds description fails to close at the same point it began, it is not valid.

12. C   Deeds must be in writing. They do not require the signature of the grantee. They do not need to be recorded to be valid, only to provide notice of the transfer.

13. B   There are 43,560 square feet in an acre.

14. B   Marketable title generally means acceptable to a reasonable buyer or lender; therefore, marketable title can readily be resold or mortgaged.

15. C   These are some of the covenants in a general warranty deed.

16. D   A deed does not have to be recorded to be valid.

17. A   A plat, which is a map used for referencing subdivision lots, is not relevant to a metes and bounds description.

18. A   A deed conveys real property.

19. C   Under foreclosure, there is not voluntary alienation of the property. In such cases, the alienation is involuntary.

20. B   The summary is called an abstract.

21. B   His claim is considered a cloud on the title and therefore it is the title insurance company's responsibility to clear it.

22. B   Real property transferred at death is a devise.

23. D   A plat is a map that may contain legal descriptions of many parcels on the map.

24. C   There are 640 acres in one section.

25. A   The links in the chain of title are the deeds connecting each successive owner to his or her interest in the property.

26. B   Intestate means a person has died without leaving a valid will.

27. C   The recording of the deed claims nothing regarding the research of past claims and interests affecting the quality of title.

28. C   Johnson does not need to show Green's permission; if Green had given permission, then the use would not be adverse.

29. B   This defines a bona fide purchaser.

30. C   The grantee is not required to be competent, although competency is desirable.

31. A   The sheriff's deed is the deed used in foreclosure sales.

32. D   The lender is the mortgagee. Therefore, this policy is the one that will insure the lender against defects in the title.

33. D   The term "probate" refers to the process of court supervision; therefore, this term would not describe Lupe's role.

34. D   Under the government rectangular survey system, ranges are referenced east or west of a principal meridian.

35. C   The recipient is the grantee.

36. D   Nothing has officially occurred regarding the transfer until delivery and acceptance of the deed.

37. D   The laws of descent determine the order of distribution of property to heirs of one who has died without leaving a valid will. A personal representative is appointed by a court to supervise the estate during probate when there is no will.

38. D   Metes and bounds descriptions are valid for legal documents.

39. D   Any transfer of title to real property is called alienation.

40. C   This is a typical example of a land description using the U.S. Rectangular Survey System.

41. A   Wilson is demanding title insurance, which insures the policy owner against financial loss if title to the real estate is not good.

42. B   The reference is to previously recorded documents such as plat maps, and not just those in the possession of the grantor.

43. D   Because the title policy here is only for the amount of the loan, it is protecting the lender or mortgagee. If the policy amount had been $125,000, it would have indicated that it was protecting Bernstein, the owner. Bernstein is not indicated to be either a lessee or a contract buyer.

44. C   A township contains 36 square miles.

45. D   A conveyance by deed is a voluntary transfer during one's lifetime.

46. D   Revenue stamps, in Michigan are calculated at $8.60 per $1,000 based on the sale price. $8.60 x 158 = $1,358.80

Real Estate Finance

1. A   The interest is taken out of the payment first and any remainder is applied to reduce the principal balance.

2. B   The alienation clause is also called a due-on-sale clause, which allows the lender the option of making the loan due and payable in full when the property is sold.

3. A   Strict foreclosure has been substantially replaced by judicial and non-judicial foreclosure.

4. C   A deed in lieu of foreclosure would not eliminate junior liens; the lender would still be encumbered by those liens.

5. B   The acceleration clause allows the lender to claim the entire balance due and payable immediately.

6. B   All real estate loans originated by state-chartered lenders are covered under this act.

7. C   The original amount loaned is the principal.

8. C   Because the seller still owes the mortgage balance that the buyer is taking over, the balance would be reflected as a debit on the seller's statement.

9. A   VA guarantees repayment as opposed to insuring the loan.

10. D   A purchase money mortgage may be a first mortgage. Additionally, a purchase money mortgage may be a junior mortgage. It is financing between the buyer and seller so it may be whatever they agree to.

11. C   Title does not have to be free and clear; that is, it may already be encumbered, in which case the new mortgage or deed of trust would simply be junior to the senior lien.

12. A   The lender is also the beneficiary.

13. A   The secondary mortgage market makes it possible for lenders to sell their loans to replenish their cash, giving them liquidity.

14. B   The release of liability makes this a novation.

15. D   New financing is the most common way to fund the a purchase of real estate.

16. A   The right of assignment addresses the lender's right to assign the loan to a new lender. This does not affect the borrower's right, if any, to an assumption.

17. C   The note is the evidence of debt and plan for repayment.

18. C   The statutory redemption period begins at the foreclosure sale and will vary depending on the type of foreclosure and the equitable redemption time.

19. B   Mitchell is still liable unless she has been released of liability; this release would involve a novation, a release of liability or a full payoff of the debt.

20. A   Even though the collateral has been taken, there may still be a deficiency judgment taken for any shortfall. This would be an unsecured lien against the debtor.

21. C   A REIT would more likely originate its own loans and investments directly.

22. D   MSHDA sets income limits each time the money is issued.

23. A   Removal of a lien is usually called a release.

24. A   Because the balance is being paid off early, the lender may be entitled to a prepayment penalty.

25. D   Under Michigan law a mortgage broker does not loan money but puts the borrower and the lender together for a fee.

26. B The lender, in this case Ace, is the mortgagee (the recipient of the mortgage instrument).

27. B FHLMC was the most recent to be created by Congress and was specifically established to provide liquidity in conventional loans, although FHLMC is now involved in the purchase and sale of FHA and VA loans as well.

28. D The numbering of liens is for identification of priority in the event of default on any or all of them.

29. A The concept of financing is to borrow money for the purchase of real property. Most buyers do not have the reserves to pay cash. for property.

30. B The mortgage represents the security for payment of the note.

31. B The power of sale allows the lender to bypass court proceedings and proceed with non-judicial foreclosure by filing the notice of default and beginning the advertisement of the foreclosure sale.

32. C This is the protection of a defeasance clause.

33. B This is the definition of a mortgage broker.

34. A This describes a deed of trust with three parties involved.

35. C The withdrawal of funds to higher yielding investments is known as disintermediation.

36. C A borrower who has hypothecated collateral does not give up possession of the collateral.

37. D Financing for vacant land is not covered under Michigan's Mortgage Brokers, Lenders, and Servicers Licensing Act.

38. B Mortgages are purchased and sold in the secondary mortgage market.

39. C The purpose of recordings is to provide notice. The lien is perfectly valid against the mortgagor without recording, but it is ineffective against third parties without providing notice.

40. D "Judicial" means "involving the court". Judicial foreclosure is required in several states to protect a borrower's rights. Unless the mortgage documents state otherwise, judicial foreclosure is not required in Michigan.

41. D   Equitable redemption allows the borrower to redeem the property by paying the principal debt in full as well as any additional interest and the costs of the sale.

42. C   GNMA is a federal agency and has been since its inception. Ginnie Mae is limited to purchasing FHA and VA loans.

43. A   Loans that meet the standards of the secondary mortgage organizations are conforming loans. A nonconforming loan typically has a higher interest rate and more stringent terms because it cannot be purchased or sold in the secondary market and therefore is less liquid.

Real Estate Appraisal

1. B   Annual net income divided by the capitalization rate = value is the correct application of the capitalization formula. (value X capitalization rate = annual net income)

2. B   Functional obsolescence refers to flawed or faulty property, rendered inferior because of advances and change.

3. A   A limited real estate appraiser is only allowed to appraise properties not involved in federally related transactions according to Michigan law.

4. C   Vacant land generally does not generate income and is therefore least likely to be appraised by the income approach.

5. C   Because of the active market and volume of transactions, comparisons under the market data approach are usually easy to find and analyze.

6. D   Wear and tear describes physical deterioration and is a result of lack of upkeep of the property.

7. B   This describes the property's utility.

8. C   Objectivity is an important factor in arriving at the estimated value of a property.

9. D   The most detailed approach is the quantity survey method, which counts every single item in the construction.

10. B   These studies do not result in an estimate of value and are therefore referred to as evaluations of the property.

11. D   Because the hospital does not have an active market for comparison and generally would not generate income in the traditional real estate investment sense, the cost approach would be the most applicable.

12. A   Because one cannot change the location of the real estate or change the uses of surrounding property, economic obsolescence is always incurable.

13. C   The assessed value of a property would be most relevant as it is used to determine the taxable value of property which may then be used to raise tax revenue for the city or county.

14. D   The major purpose for appraisals of properties in the residential resale market is for mortgage loan financing.

15. A   The greater the risk, the greater the potential reward (rate of return).

16. B   Valuation is the determination of a probable price whereas evaluation is not.

17. C   Effective demand combines want and need with financial ability to satisfy those needs. In this case, despite the needs or desires of the marketplace, few people can afford or qualify for the available financing, therefore in this situation effective demand for the property is negatively effected.

18. D   Condemnation value is the value placed upon private property which the government is taking for public use by the power of eminent domain. Condemnation value is the amount that the government must pay for the condemned property and should reflect fair market value.

19. C   Highest and best use is the feasible use of property that results in the greatest present value.

20. B   This illustrates the principle of substitution, indicating that the highest value of a property has a tendency to be established by the cost of purchasing or constructing another property of equal utility and desirability.

21. D   Depreciation is the loss in value of real property from any cause.

22. C   An appraisal is an estimate or opinion of value.

23. A   Demand, utility, scarcity, and transferability are the legal and economic characteristics which must be present for real property to have value.

24. C   A CMA does not require an appraisal license. A license is now required for appraisals done for lending purposes. A CMA does examine properties sold.

25. D According to the contribution principle, the value of an improvement is measured according to its contribution to the value of the entire property. In this case, the presence of the fireplace can be valued at $1,100.

26. D The narrative appraisal recounts all of the research, substantiation, and logic of the appraisal process and therefore is the most comprehensive.

27. C Although these faucets may be operable and even in good physical condition, this design is outdated and is no longer desirable; therefore, this demonstrates functional obsolescence.

28. A This illustrates the principle of anticipation, which recognizes that property value is based on the expectation of future benefits of ownership. Appraisers must stay abreast of market conditions and change in order to anticipate their impact on value.

29. B Market value is based upon the parties being equally motivated. If the seller must sell quickly and is willing to accept any price, the sale price will not reflect market value.

30. A Race is not a valid element of the analysis.

31. B Effective age refers to the age that the structure appears to be. Therefore, the maintenance and improvements would be an attempt to extend the effective useful life of the property and would have an impact on the effective age, not the actual age of the property.

32. C In this case appraisers would probably use replacement cost to create a similar structure employing current building materials and methods of construction.

33. D An overimprovement is also termed a superadequacy.

34. C The lower the supply of a product (scarcity), the higher its price (and vice versa), which illustrates one aspect of the concept of supply and demand.

35. C The gross rent multiplier (GRM) uses gross income, not taking vacancy or operating expenses into consideration. The cap rate uses net income which includes operating expenses.

36. B Michigan law allows licenses to be obtained in several occupations by satisfying the respective requirements of each license. It is important for a real estate licensee to avoid a conflicts of interest when holding more than one license. A licensee should not appraise property in a transaction he is involved with as an agent.

37. A   Hazard insurance value would not include the land because land typically would not be damaged in the event of a hazard.

38. D   Book value would determine the adjusted basis of the property for depreciation purposes, which would be relevant for the preparation of income taxes.

39. C   Jennings will not be able to transfer the property to an otherwise willing buyer for another year due to the option he sold to another individual. If the option is exercised, the maximum value received will be the option price, which will be below market price.

Land Use Controls

1. C   Subdivisions in which the lots are five acres or more are exempt from the Interstate Land Sales Full Disclosure Act.

2. C   The federal Interstate Sales Full Disclosure Act regulates interstate sale of unimproved lots. The sale of lots may be additionally regulated on a local level by city code, but it is the Interstate Land Sales Full Disclosure Act that requires this specific documentation.

3. A   These restrictions are called restrictive covenants. They preserve and protect the quality of land in the subdivision and maximize the value of the land by guarding its use.

4. B   The state legislature passes enabling acts, based upon the police power of government, that allow lower levels of government to pass ordinances which provide for planning and zoning to protect the health, safety, and welfare of the people.

5. D   Suit to quiet title is a remedy for a problem with the ownership of the property and is not a violation of a zoning law.

6. D   Building codes are rules set by government to regulate building and construction standards.

7. C   This act is called SARA, the Superfund Amendments and Reauthorization Act. SARA amended the 1976 act referred to as CERCLA, the Comprehensive Environmental Response, Compensation and Liability Act.

8. A   City certification allows a government to inspect properties when ownership is being transferred to assure that the building is up to code. The number of occupants is not a code requirement.

9. A   An injunction is the legal action whereby the court issues an instruction to discontinue a specified activity.

10. D   If spot zoning of a property is solely for the benefit of the property owner and has the effect of increasing the land value, the rezoning is illegal and invalid.

11. C   The Interstate Land Sales Full Disclosure Act regulates developers of subdivisions of 25 or more lots sold across state lines.

12. C   A variance is a permitted deviation from specific requirements of a zoning ordinance, which is a form of public land use control.

13. B   Although planning and zoning proposals may be presented to property owners in a community, unanimous consent of all owners is typically not required.

14. D   The certificate of occupancy is issued after a satisfactory final inspection and permits occupancy of the property.

15. C   The term "spot zoning" refers to a specific property within a zoned area that has been rezoned to permit a use different from the zoning requirements for that area.

16. C   Subdivision regulations are established so that a new development will not require additional services that would place an undue burden on the surrounding community.

17. C   Enforcement of covenants is not restricted to the original owners but runs with the land to all subsequent owners.

18. D   Michigan's Wetland Protection Act requires a permit to dredge in a designated wetland.

19. C   The Resource Conversation and Recovery Act (RCRA), and not CERCLA, defines hazardous waste.

20. C   The term "variance" is used to indicate that permission has been granted by zoning authorities to deviate from the zoning code. Variances are permitted where the deviation is not substantial and where an undue hardship has been created for the property owner.

21. A   When restrictive covenants surpass the zoning regulations they may be implemented. If these covenants are less restrictive than the zoning ordinances, the zoning requirements prevail.

22. B   If a subdivision is in a zoned area, restrictive covenants have priority over zoning ordinances – providing the covenants are more restrictive, are recorded and are legal.

23. D   Zoning ordinances consist of the zoning map and the text of the zoning ordinance. The zoning map divides the community into various designated districts, and the text of the zoning ordinance sets forth the type of usage permitted and restricted under each zoning classification.

24. C   Zoning laws set certain standards for setbacks that must be met in each permitted type of use.

25. D   Variances are permitted when the deviation is minimal and would not impact the neighborhood, and where strict compliance to the restriction would cause undue hardship to the owner.

Encumbrances and Government Restrictions

1. B   A bailment is created when personal property is delivered to another who becomes responsible for it.

2. D   The gradual build up of land due to changes in a watercourse over time by deposits of silt, sand and gravel is the definition of accretion.

3. C   "Intestate" is a term that refers to an owner who dies without having a valid will.

4. B   In addition to maximizing land values, restrictive covenants also preserve and protect the quality of land.

5. C   Easements may be granted by the courts when a property owner has no access to roads and is landlocked.

6. A   The land that benefits from the easement appurtenant is called the dominant tenement or the dominant estate.

7. C   The only method to accurately determine the existence of an encroachment is by a survey of the boundary line.

8. B   Jack has a temporary privilege known as a license.

9. A   An easement appurtenant attaches to the land and follows the transfer of title to land from one owner to another. This is called running with the land.

10. C   Escheat is the government's right to private property that is left by someone who has died intestate and without locatable heirs.

11. A   General liens are claims against a person and all of their property.

12. C   When property is condemned under eminent domain, the property owner is compensated.

13. D   Compensation is the critical factor in determining the difference between police power and eminent domain. In a police power action, such as the creation of zoning ordinances, no compensation is paid in the event of loss by affected property owners. Under eminent domain the owner is compensated for their loss.

14. A   The term "appurtenances" refers to automatic rights that are a natural consequence of owning property.

15. A   The governmental power through which title to property reverts to the state when heirs to the property cannot be found is known as escheat.

16. D   Mechanic's liens usually receive preferential treatment because of their special priority, not because of the type of documentation, the amount of the debt, or any penalties assessed.

17. B   Easements by condemnation are created by exercise of the government's right of eminent domain. Through this power, the government can take title to land and take the right to use land for some purpose in the future.

18. D   A notice of commencement is a formal notice that work is beginning on the property. It notifies everyone involved of the name and address of the owner for the purpose of serving proper legal notice.

19. A   Income tax is a general lien (a claim against all assets) and not a specific lien.

20. A   After an uninterrupted period of time (determined by law) and open and continued use, the city of New York could claim that the center's sidewalk belongs to the city via easement by prescription. By interrupting use of the sidewalks once a year, Rockefeller Center ensures that a claim of easement by prescription would not be valid.

21. A   Eminent domain is characterized by two limitations: The condemned property must be for the use and benefit of the general public, and property owners must be paid the fair market value of the property lost.

22. B   Authorized use of another's property is called an easement.

23. D   An easement or right-of-way can be created by law, by use, or by humans. It can be negative or affirmative. It can also be commercial in nature – owned by the government, an agency of the government, or a public utility.

24. B   A profit a prendre is salable, inheritable, and transferable. It is the right to take products of the soil from the land of another.

25. A   Restrictive covenants are private restrictions on ownership.

26. B   Unless otherwise noted, assessed values are 50 percent of the property's market value in Michigan.

27. D   An encumbrance is anything that lessens the bundle of rights in real property, but a lien is a special type of encumbrance that is a claim against another's property. Therefore, a deed restriction, which is a limitation on land use appearing on the deed, is not a lien, but it is an encumbrance that affects the property owner's use.

28. D   A lis pendens (from Latin, "pending litigation") is a notice to the world that a lawsuit has been filed and is awaiting trial concerning a specific property.

29. A   Construction liens must be filed within 90 days. Court proceedings must be brought within 360 days after the lien was recorded.

30. A   A special assessment is a specific lien against the property to collect payment for a share of the cost of an improvement made to the property, usually by a government agency, such as a municipality.

31. A   Common appurtenant rights would not include condemnation, which is a term that refers to a government power under eminent domain. However, profit a prendre, license and air rights are common appurtenant rights; that is, rights that are a natural consequence of property ownership.

32. D   Restrictions on a private owner's use of land by a non-governmental entity are known as restrictive covenants.

33. D   Riparian rights describe the rights of owners whose land borders flowing bodies of water.

34. A   Dedication is a common practice whereby a developer sets aside a portion of the land in a subdivision for uses such as a park, a common area, etc.

35. D   Riparian rights belong to the owner of property bordering a flowing body of water.

Leasehold Estates

1. A   To form a contract there must be consideration. In a lease contract the consideration is the rent.

2. A   This describes an estate from year to year (periodic estate), which continues for an additional period if no notice is given, a periodic tenancy terminates only with notice.

3. B   A security deposit is intended to ensure the return of the premises in good repair.

4. B   The landlord (the party transferring the right to possession) is the lessor.

5. D   Jenkins has an estate for years, for which no notice to terminate is required.

6. A   A gross lease has a fixed rental amount for the full term and does not address future rent increases.

7. C   Assignment or subleasing is allowed unless the lease agreement prohibits doing so.

8. B   The sale and leaseback allows a tenant (former owner) to free up capital by selling the property while still maintaining possession.

9. D   This describes a net lease.

10. A   This tenant is holding over and the landlord has the right to evict the tenant or renew the lease.

11. D   A ground lease usually involves a very long term because there is typically going to be construction on the leased property.

12. D   Freehold would describe the interest of an owner, not a renter.

13. C   Negligence does not constitute a termination of the lease.

14. D   A lease requires the term and conditions of termination.

15. A   One would not negotiate an estate at sufferance. It would exist only after one of the other estates terminated without the tenant properly vacating.

16. A   Oral leases are acceptable for terms of less than one year. Therefore, oral leases are valid. The Statute of Frauds also allows short-term oral leases to be enforceable in court.

17. B   With an estate at will, there is no formal agreement regarding the termination except the need to provide notice.

18. D   This right states that the landlord is allowed to enter the premises only in emergency situations and not at will.

19. C   The lease contract has the most influence in determining the rights and duties of landlord and tenant.

20. C   If the landlord or tenant breaches the contract, the term of the lease may be reduced.

21. A   Possession of the property will revert to the lessor (the landlord).

22. C   Eviction is the proper legal process for removing a tenant.

23. B   In an estate for years the termination date is stipulated in the lease and does not require notice by either party to terminate.

24. D   The leaky gas heater is the most severe of these problems and must be repaired for the property to remain habitable.

25. A   This contract is a lease.

Property Management

1. A   Aside from the obligations created under the property management contract; there are no policies for management set by either law or Boards of REALTORS®.

2. D   Extended coverage provides protection for loss due to these additional hazards.

3. C   Budgeting for this kind of upkeep is an attempt to avoid problems before they arise; therefore, this is preventative maintenance.

4. B   A regional shopping mall usually has several anchor tenants.

5. C   In many cases a residential manager is not able to represent the owner in court cases such as evictions.

6. D   The operating budget addresses the shortest period of time, typically one year.

7. B   The management proposal is the first step in a property management relationship.

8. A   A tenant does not have a legitimate financial interest in the land. The tenant's interest is limited to a possessory right.

9. D   The shopping center would not likely have a resident manager.

10. A   The strip shopping center needs visibility for the tenants. The other properties usually have greater exposure because of their large size and the presence of one or more anchor tenants.

11. D   Because collections do not vary as much in the case of for homeowners' associations, the manager would not likely be compensated with a percentage of these collections. In this case, the percentage method would not be reflective of the manager's performance.

12. C   Preservation of the value and quality of the property is the major function of a property manager.

13. C   Corrective maintenance is performed only as needed and is not predictable.

Taxation

1. B   Discount points may be deductible in the purchase of a personal residence.

2. C   The tax basis for all real property received by heirs is the market value of the property on the date of the decedent's death.

3. B   The Taxpayer Relief Act of 1997 allows a first-time buyer to withdraw $10,000 from a retirement program without paying the penalty.

4. D   They are deductible against the price and profit of that property, not against other income.

5. B   Sale of new cooperatives is selling shares of stock and is therefore considered selling securities under Michigan's Uniform Securities Act.

6. D   The Taxpayer Relief Act of 1997 allows a person to claim the universal exclusion if he can show that the property was his primary residence for 2 of the last 5 years.

7. D   The principal repaid on a loan is not deductible.

8. C $68,500 cost + $12,000 pool + $7,500 room addition = $88,000 adjusted basis.

9. B   On a rental property, there is no rollover provision.

10. A   The 1997 Taxpayer's Relief Act eliminated the time frame to roll over the sale proceeds on a primary residence.

11. D   The taxpayer is taxed only on the profit, or gain, from the sale and not on the price or net proceeds. The gain would be taxed over $500,000 if they are a married couple.

12. D $72,000 cost + $14,500 pool + $7,200 room addition = $493,700 adjusted basis. $149,000 sale price - $93,700 adjusted basis = $55,300 gain.

13. C $69,000 cost + $12,000 room addition = $81,000 adjusted basis. $121,000 sale price - $81,000 adjusted basis - $40,000 gain. $168,900 new home - $40,000 deferred gain = $128,900 adjusted basis in the new home.

Review Exam

1. B   Security are the property of the tenant. The landlord is required to return the security deposit to the tenant at the end of the lease unless there is damage to the unit beyond normal wear and tear or there are utility bills or rents still owed by the tenant.

2. B   Public Act 299 is known as the Occupational Code.

3. B   Only a court of law can send a person to prison. The department can only impose the penalties to discipline a licensee under the guidelines of Article 6 of the Occupational Code.

4. C   According to the Out of State Land Sales Rules, the Michigan broker is responsible for all expenses incurred by the Department to investigate out of state land sales.

5. B   The only property a licensees can advertise in their own name is their principal residence. Licensees can sell their principal residence 'by owner' without going through a broker.

6. A   A salesperson's license is delivered to the employing broker, who is responsible for the licensee's wall license. It must be conspicuously displayed in the brokers' office.

7. D   All earnest money deposits must be delivered to the broker. The broker is responsible for depositing all earnest money received into a trust account.

8. A   The Michigan Land Sales Act states that a purchaser must receive a copy of the property report and have ample time to review it prior to being bound to a purchase agreement.

9. C A principal associate broker is responsible for the actions of the firm. Therefore, when that person is no longer connected with the firm, their license is automatically suspended. A principal associate broker license is not transferable.

10. B The employing broker has custody of the license which must be conspicuously displayed in the broker's place of business. The licensee has a pocket card as proof of licensing.

11. C The Notice of Furnishing is one of four documents required under the Michigan Construction Lien Act.

12. A MSHDA financing must be used for the purchase of a principal residence only.

13. D Michigan's law can only apply to state chartered lenders.

14. D A real estate company always has a right to know what compensation they will receive as a result of participating in a real estate transaction with another firm.

15. C Dredging is the removing of soil or minerals from a wetland and is prohibited without a permit from the Michigan Department of Environmental Quality (DEQ).

16. B Mortgage Lender. Although a mortgage banker may perform the same function as a mortgage lender, a mortgage banker is not defined in the Michigan Mortgage Brokers, Lenders and Servicers Licensing Act.

17. A Michigan usury law does not permit an interest rate over 11% for private parties and other unregulated lenders.

18. D A licensee is only allowed to advertise in the name under which the license is issued.

19. D A licensee can only accept a commission or valuable consideration from their employing broker.

20. A It is not necessary to file a new application to renew a license.

21. D A seller must disclose the proximity of a farm, farm operation, landfill, airport or shooting range according to the Sellers Disclosure Act.

22. D The earnest money deposit must be deposited in the broker's trust account within two banking days from the broker's knowledge of an accepted

agreement. The broker is the custodian of the funds for the transaction. Therefore, the law is very strict about how the earnest money is handled.

23. C   If a landlord posts a bond with the Secretary of State, he can access the security deposits that are in the property management account.

24. B   It is the brokers' obligation to return the licensee's wall license to the Department by certified mail within five days of when the licensee leaves the company.

25. C   Licensees must carry their pocket card whenever they are acting in the capacity of that license. Since it is true that you can act as a real estate agent in a variety of circumstances, so it is wise to carry your pocket card as often as you would carry your drivers' license.

26. A   A licensee must disclose their licensure when they are interested in purchasing the property and must disclose in writing that they are licensed.

27. A   A landlord cannot can not include any provision in a lease that holds the landlord harmless for negligence and relieves him from liability for that negligence.

28. C   If the owner has stated that no one can view the property at this time then, it is not an act in violation of Fair Housing Law to refuse to show it to anyone. A licensee must obey all reasonable and legal instructions from the seller.

29. B   Occupation is not a protected classification.

30. B   The seller is responsible for the Michigan Transfer Tax, however, the buyer and seller can negotiate who will actually pay the fee.

31. A   The person who hires another to represent their interest is the principal/client.

32. C   The person who holds the position of trust in an agency relationship is the fiduciary. The terms "fiduciary" and "trust" are synonymous.

33. B   The exclusive right-to-sell listing entitles the broker to a commission no matter who sells the listing and therefore offers the greatest protection for a broker.

34. A   This type of listing allows many brokers to be under contract with the same owner.

35. B   A Bill of Sale is the document that is used for the transfer of personal property. A deed only transfers title to real property.

36. D   The only protection Broker Jones would have as a claim for his commission is in the carryover provision.

37. B   6% of $100,000 = $6,000. 3% of $19,900 = $697. $6,000 + $697 = $6,697.

38. C   7% of $5,000 = $350.

39. A   Dual Agency, by definition, is the representation by one company of both the buyer and seller in the same transaction. Therefore if the broker does not allow agents to represent both parties in a transaction, the broker does not allow dual agency.

40. C   Only an employing broker can compensate its agents.

41. A   The common law of agency gives the most limited authority to special agents which most accurately describes the relationship between the broker and the buyer or seller.

42. B   A Quit Claim Deed gives no guarantees or warrantees to the grantee and therefore provides the least protection to the grantee.

43. B   Ownership of time intervals is the definition of time-sharing condominiums.

44. A   The grantor is the seller. Under a Warranty Deed the grantor is making the most ~~many~~ promises, warrantees and promises to the grantee and therefore provides the least protection for the grantor.

45. A   Accretion is the gradual build up or addition to the land by the movement of water.

46. C   The document that gives the complete history of the property including the chain of title AND encumbrances is the abstract.

47. D   The grantee is the purchaser. Grantees do not sign the deed.

48. C   "Indefeasible" means "cannot be defeated." Therefore, title that is indefeasible can not be voided.

49. A   The holder of a life estate can not create an interest in land beyond their death. Therefore Mr. Hearns' leasehold interest would be terminated.

50. A   Land that is transferred by a property owner to the government creates an easement by grant and is known as dedication. This is most often seen in subdivision development.

51. D   If a person dies without a will or locatable heirs, the government becomes the "heir" of the estate by the power of escheat.

52. D   Tenancy by the entirety requires the unity of person. Michigan views ownership by a husband and wife as ownership by one "person." They obtained that status through marriage.

53. C   The bylaws of the condominium set forth the operative rules. They set forth the guidelines to be followed by all co-owners to maintain the highest value for the complex.

54. A   Quit Claim Deeds give no promises or guarantees. They will, however, transfer whatever interest the grantor had in the property at the time of execution.

55. A   The deed would be invalid. The grantee must be named with certainty and is an essential element of a valid deed.

56. D   Basically, a tenant at sufferance is occupying a piece of property without the legal right to do so and therefore has the least bundle of rights.

57. C   Fee simple estates contain the most complete bundle of rights and are therefore the most freely transferable and inheritable.

58. A   Household furnishings are readily moveable and are therefore personal property.

59. D   In a net lease the tenant pays all or a portion of the operating expenses in addition to a monthly rental amount. Mortgage debt service is the responsibility of the owner and is not considered an operating expense.

60. C   Most contracts, including lease contracts, are not terminated by the death of either party.

61. B   The Statute of Frauds states that contracts that create or transfer an interest in real property must be in writing to be enforceable.

62. D   During the term of the land contract, the vendee has a legally recognized interest in the property known as equitable title. At the end of the contract the vendee receives legal title.

63. A   This Michigan law will also protect the buyer if the property is taken under eminent domain between the purchase agreement and the closing.

64. C   Money presented with the offer to purchase is known as earnest money. Earnest money is not required by law. Its intent is to demonstrate good faith and the financial ability of the buyer to complete the purchase.

65. B   Specific performance is a court remedy which protects the purchaser in the event of default by the seller.

66. B   Valuable consideration is anything based on money and is an essential element of all contracts including options.

67. C   The contract is voidable by the minor only.

68. B   At the end of the lease the right of possession will revert back to the owner.

69. A   Amortization is the repayment of a financial obligation in regular installments which include repayment of the principal and interest.

70. B   Financing which includes the real property as well as items of personal property is known as a package mortgage.

71. C   FHA and VA do not loan money. FHA insures loans, and VA guarantees loans which are given through participating lenders.

72. B   The Federal Housing Authority, an agency of the Department of Housing and Urban Development (HUD), was created for the purpose of insuring loans.

73. A   When a mortgage is assumed, a new mortgage is not being created, therefore The Federal Truth-in-Lending law does not apply.

74. D   Mortgagee. The lender is the giver of the loan and the receiver of the mortgage which places a lien on the property.

75. A   In order to qualify for a VA mortgage, the Veterans Administration requires a veteran to prove their eligibility with this certificate.

76. C $.0075 times $20,000 = $150. 360 divided by 12 months = $30. $54 divided by 36 months = $1.50. $150 = $30 = $1.50 = $182.

77. D $126 x 12 = $1,512 x .28 = $423.36. (This answer was rounded).

78. C   One point is one percent of the loan amount. $90,000 x 1% = $900. 4 points x $900 = $3,600.

79. D   Hypothecation is pledging real property as security for the debt while retaining possession of the property.

80. B   A vendee is one who buys or offers to buy as in a land contract.

81. B   This is accomplished within one transaction. The terms of the purchase and the leaseback are negotiated and agreed to at the same time and in the same instrument.

82. B   This law is designed to protect people who finance the purchase of residential property and therefore are not involved in financing on a regular basis.

83. A   This clause gives the lender the right to begin foreclosure proceedings when the borrower is in default by 'accelerating' the term of the mortgage making the balance due immediately.

84. A   This court proceeding is most common when there is an undisclosed heir or lien on title. It is also used in adverse possession cases.

85. B   Physical deterioration is depreciation in value due to wear and tear. Physical deterioration may be curable or incurable depending upon the cost and the possibility to cure. It becomes incurable when the cost to cure is greater than the final value, or when the improvement is impossible to complete.

86. B   Non-conforming use. Continuing the non-conforming use is subject to the guidelines set forth by the municipality granting the non-conforming use.

87. C   Setback requirements. Setbacks also dictate how far the building must be from the side and rear lot lines.

88. B   One mile square is 640 acres. A half mile SQUARE is a quarter section or 160 acres.

89. D   Real property taxes are considered recorded when they are assessed so they generally are the first lien on the property.

90. C   Properties that are outdated, outmoded, or no longer desirable due to obsolete mechanical or structural items or design are considered functionally obsolete.

91. A   Because of real property's physical characteristic of immobility, location has the greatest affect on value.

92. C   Police power is the government's right to do whatever is necessary to protect the health, safety and welfare of the public. This includes local government's right to pass zoning ordinances.

93. D   Governments have the right to take private land for public use. The government must show a benefit to the general public to legally use their power of eminent domain.

94. D   The owner must apply for a zoning variance because the owner wants to do something different than the current zoning.

95. D   Regulations setting forth acceptable building methods and materials are known as building codes. Building codes vary across the United States.

96. B   Zoning that would permit a use that is contrary to current zoning and would benefit the property owner is spot zoning. Spot zoning can be legal and valid or illegal and invalid.

97. A   Lis pendens is a notice that there is a pending lawsuit involving a specific property. This notice "reserves" the priority of a claim on the property in the event the plaintiff is successful in their lawsuit.

98. D   All of the answer selections are encumbrances. Only the mortgage creates a lien.

99. C   This scenario is an example of block busting.

100. B   Under the Civil Rights Act of 1866 race is the only protected classification.